Work In Movies?

Are You Crazy?

By Tim Cooney c.a.s.

Dedication

For my wife Cherry who has given me a new life
Also to my mom because well she is mom
and finally to Charlie and Helayna who have always made me
laugh

Contents

Preface

After working in the motion picture and television business for over 30 years' people I talk to ask the same question. How can I get into the film business? Or I have a relative who wants to work in the film business how did you get into the business? That particular answer isn't really relevant in today's film business. How I did it would not work today. The business has changed dramatically in the last ten years and I will touch briefly on those changes. Back when I started you usually worked for one studio and retired there. The whole pension system is based on working 30 years 2000 hours a year and having 60 thousand hours accumulated to get your full pension. Back when you worked at one studio this was common. After the studio system broke up it is difficult to get that 2000 hours a year. In the late seventies the studio system broke up and the only way to get a job was to hustle and hope your reputation preceded you. When you worked at a studio you would work in a position for a while and when the opportunity arose you were then moved up to a new position. Today with all the film schools out there people are coming into the business at all levels from all over the country. In this book we will talk about film schools' verses on the job training. We will talk about the most asked questions "do I have to know somebody to get into the film business?" Do I have to go to a film school? Should I lie on my resume? Read the book and these questions will be answered.

The film business used to be a good job and in some cases it still is. With so many nonunion shows going on and filming in other states it is a lot easier to get work. With the pressures put on everybody to do the job right and on time the business has changed for the worst. Show business used to bring to the imagination glamour and the thoughts of premiers and parties. In today's entertainment field it is the business of show not show business. Today accountants and agents run studios and film makers have a harder time getting pictures made. You don't shoot movies you shoot schedules. Now the competition for a job is fierce. Many times you are not judged on what you can do or even what you have done. But who you know. Many times you will work 12 to 14 hours a day and if you have a family kiss them good-bye until the end of the season. Contrary to popular belief it is not all autographs and sunglasses. But if you are like the majority of people who want to be in the business any negative things I say won't deter you. So just like the rest of us welcome you are in good company. So push on and move forward people like me have been trying to retire for years and maybe before I go we will work together.

Chapter 1

Pep Talk

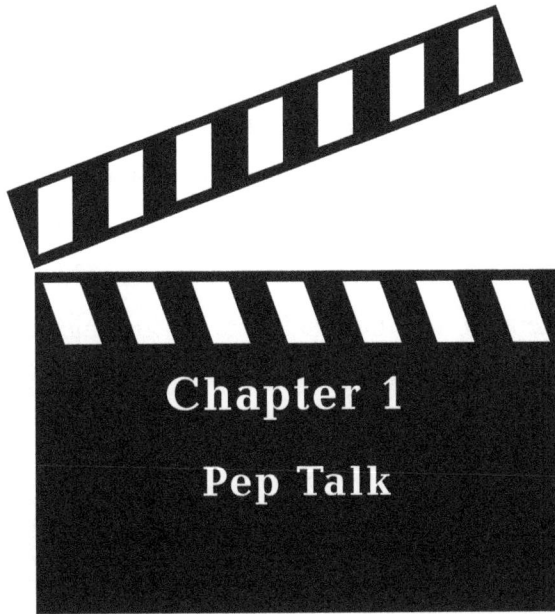

O k, here is the pep talk. The business is set up so you will fail. If you get lucky and DON'T GIVE UP you will succeed. It is hard to get into the union. It is hard to get into the department you want to work in. It is hard to get to know the people you need to know to succeed. It is damn near impossible to get your first job and really difficult to get jobs after that. How's the pep talk going so far?

You must keep trying because much of it is luck and timing. Just because you don't want to work on the crew because you are going to be a director or producer, it is important you read the entire book cover to cover. Many of the things I will tell you will apply to every department. So if you skip around you might miss the one piece of advice you need to get that all-important lucky break. Some producers will start a show nonunion. Should you happen to be on one of those shows when it goes union you automatically get in the union. In the interim they have saved money on construction and other costs. It doesn't matter to them that they have taken money from who knows how many families. It doesn't matter that they have denied those families their health benefits. Of course the stars are getting their money the producers are getting theirs. This is a very selfish business. This is the norm and not exactly the glamour you have heard about.

Lets talk about luck for a moment. Luck is important in life, but more so in the film business. Luck is more important than talent if you have both you will go far in the business. Before I start with some of the boring stuff just a little inside story you might enjoy. I was working on a picture called Demolition Man. The picture stared Sly Stallone, Wesley Snipes, and Lorie Petty. After about ten days of shooting they replaced Lorie Petty with this newcomer Sandra Bullock. I think up until then Sandra had only done 1 or maybe 2 pictures. One day we are shooting on the stage at Warner Brothers and Jan Debont comes walking on the stage. He was a DP (director of photography) at the time. I knew him from another show and asked him what he was doing here.

He said he got a break and was going to direct his first picture and he heard this new actress was pretty good. He was going to look at dailies (dailies are what we filmed the day or days before) to see how well she acted looked on film ETC. Just based on the dailies Jan hired Sandra Bullock for her breakout film Speed. So if Lorie Petty had worked out or if Sandra did not get the Demo Man job or Jan did not get his first directing gig any number of other things happened maybe Sandra Bullock would not be as big of star she is today or maybe she would have given up on acting and went on to do something else. Maybe she would have been one of those actresses you see but don't even know her name. We will never know. Luck and being in the right place gave her that opportunity. This is just one story to illustrate how important luck can play in your career. All the stories and information I am going to give you is important. Even if I am talking about acting many of those things will apply to other areas as well.

The most important word in today's film business is RELATIONSHIPS. A good example is if you know someone who has a good action movie script and you option it. By the way that means paying a fee for the rights to turn it into a film. Let's say you have a relationship with Sly Stallone and he agrees to do it. You can go to a major studio and get a deal. Out of the clear blue sky you are a producer and you went from obscurity to the limelight overnight. I know some people that this scenario happened but it is very rare. It is very difficult to the point of impossible to get a box office star to read a script from an unknown writer or producer. You have to go through their agent and the actor may never even hear about it. But if you know a box office star who will read your script and they like it you have caught the brass ring.

Relationships are more commonly important this way. You know a production manager/producer who is getting ready to do a film and he has the authority to hire you. You work in one of the crafts such as in the grip or lighting dept. (a grip is a person who handles the tracks that the camera might be on for a dolly shot. Also a grip would put nets or other diffusion in front of lights. A dolly grip is a person who pushes the dolly that the camera is attached to anyway you get the idea). A key grip or gaffer needs a crew and you have worked for them before or because he is your friend he gives you a shot.

As long as they thought your work was good and you got along well with everybody they will hire you again. A friend of yours just got a job on a picture and now you can find out the particulars about the show and go after it. As long as you know how. Maybe that friend puts in a good word for you and they hire you for almost no money. But you end up with a credit on a major film. Yes, the business is now built more on relationships than anything. So it is very important that when the opportunity arises cultivate that relationship. Make friends with everybody. Make an enemy out of nobody. In this business you never know how your next job is going to come to you. I have gotten a job because I knew an actor on the show. I lost a job because my competition was the boyfriend of a Paramount executive. The producers on the show assured me that I had the job and at the last minute the studio overruled them. That is the perfect example of the better-qualified person not getting the job because of a relationship.

The reason relationships have become so important is because the business has changed. The pressure to finish a film on time and on budget is overwhelming. Producers want to know the people they have to depend on. After all if you screw up it reflects on them. Believe me when a show is in production the last thing a producer or director wants is more problems. So as you can see relationships are as important as learning your craft.

Now I will say a few words about learning your craft. There are now so many people who instead of starting at the bottom start at the top. They go out and spend a lot of money on equipment work cheap so they can get hired. Then after that and in most cases rarely work. So start at the bottom and learn your craft. You will be respected within the business and at the same time be able to work as much as you want. There was this sound mixer who had not been mixing very long and really did not know much when it came to mixing. He was a boom man for a short time. He got this job that was shooting down south non-union. He took the job because it was a great opportunity for him. The producers hired him because they wanted a black person mixing sound. The film stared Denzel Washington and the usual sound mixer who works with Denzel either was not available or would not do it because it was non-union.

These kind of demands are normal in the business but are not talked about much. A producer will do almost anything to accommodate a box office star to keep his film on time and on schedule. Anyway this guy along with the postproduction mixers who were great won the Oscar for best sound.

Kevin Costner is getting ready to do a film the following year and says get me the production mixer who won the Oscar last year. So this guy gets hired again. Believe it or not he wins the Oscar again. That makes two years in a row. Up until then it had never been won two years in a row by a production mixer. You might be thinking how can he win the Oscar if he does not know what he is doing? In this case it isn't about how good the sound he mixed turned out because they can replace anything he did and I know they did. It's called looping and they looped a lot of both pictures. Not only did he lack the skills he needed to be a good mixer because he did not work as a cable man and boom man long enough to really learn the gig I also understand from people he worked with that he lacked the people skills needed to succeed.

People skills and diplomacy are very important in the business and always has been my biggest problem. Anyway back to the story after a few other jobs word got out and he did not work much he left the business to teach film back east. This is a guy that has two Oscars and he can't get work. So in this chapter I hope you have learned you have to have luck. You have to develop relationships. You have to learn your craft. You have to be diplomatic. You now know what a grip is. Hopefully as with the rest of this book you will act on what you have learned follow through and end up with a career in the film business. People who work in show business are the most independent people you will ever meet. People in this business would rather give up a good job than take any crap.

Now we will talk about professionalism and attitude. My attitude of course has been warped because I have been doing this for over thirty years. But I have always tried to remain professional. Keeping with that theme I will tell you the reason we shoot the same scene so many times. Many people when they come onto a set say look at all the people just standing around. They don't realize there is a group of people that prepare the scene to be shot while the actors are in makeup and wardrobe and there is a group of people that shoot the scene with the actors. So not everybody works at the same time. When you watch TV or a movie you will notice in one scene you will have wide shots and close-ups of each actor in the scene. Each one of those shots is shot separately and then given to the editor to put together. Editing is an art form and I have seen editors that saved pictures from bad directing. I have also seen editors ruin films. I have been fortunate to work with the best in the business. The best directors and the best crew. If you want to be one of the best learn your craft don't give up and be honest in all your dealings. Go for it choose your career and be the very best in that field and you will work as much as you want all over the world.

Chapter 2

You can't do it
This Way Anymore

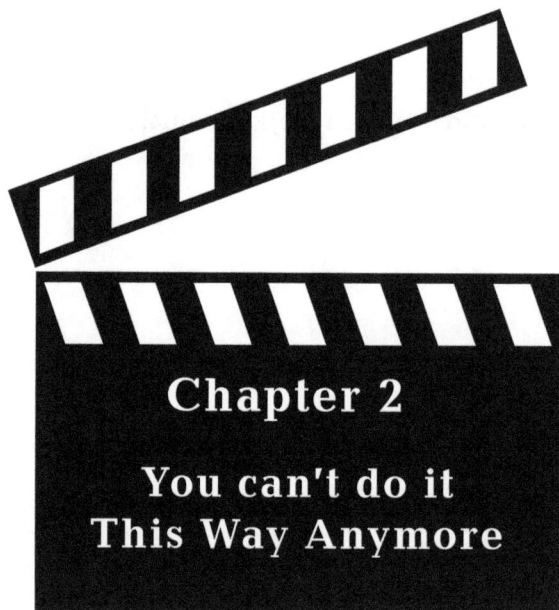

This was part of an article that I wrote. It was in an industry magazine called The Coffee Audio Files. This describes my peculiar life and how I ended up in the film business and also why you can't do it the way I did.

As I write this, the business is very slow again. The economy is so bad that the vacuum cleaner salesmen and the Jehovah Witness people are carpooling. So here is a condensed special psycho version of this is your life, Tim Cooney. So I was talking to my little brother about this book he's 6 months younger than me. No, that's not right. I come from an Italian family my mother taught me to shave. How about I was the son of a sharecropper... No even I can't sell that one. How about it all started in a small radio station in a speck of town in West Virginia. No, that's not it. Actually when I tell you how it started you will think I am making it up. But I'm not. It could only happen in Hollywood…

To say my parents were conservative would be like saying Steven Segal could use some acting lessons. A major understatement. My father was an attorney and politician. My mother was the head clerk of the draft board. It was the 60s. They were drafting everybody and once even a blind person went to Vietnam. I was a working musician; I had long hair and really did not fit in. So I ran away from home and everything I knew. My parents and most of the population of California weren't exactly sorry to see me go. I was almost 18 when I joined the circus. Yes that's right, the circus! Boy were my parents proud then. I graduated from the Ringling Bros Barnum and Baily Clown College. I was a clown on the circus. Then I learned to train elephants and big cats. My mother's therapy lasted only 5 years and my father started drinking heavily. They actually started talking to me again about a year later. Now all the jokes that go with me being in the circus with clowns, animals, ect, are too easy so I won't go there. Just pause a minute and make up your own we will wait.…

As your reading this you are thinking what the hell has all this got to do with the film business. Well here it comes this is how I got to where I am today, wherever that is. Back in 1975 I was hired by Tippi Hedron to train Elephants for a movie she and her husband Noel were going to make, a film called Roar. I was doing the elephant show at the St. Louis Zoo at the time, but was ready to move back to California. Not only was it my first movie it was also the first for many guys that went on to have successful careers. Mr. Warmth DP and director Jan Debont, it was his first American film. It was also Melanie Griffiths second or third film. The sound mixer Courtney Goodin had done other films, but he and many of the guys were doing this to get into the union. The DP Alan Caso was an operator on this film and many more, to numerous to name. My first day on that set I guarantee you was not like anybody else's first day in the business.

The film set and compound were in Soledad Canyon in Acton, California. I was finished working with the elephants around 9 am. The other animal Handlers, who took care of the 100+ cats were also done with their chores. These cats had never been trained and I was told they were all hand raised. Gee, that made me feel better. 300 lb cats that are already used to the people they want to eat. With the exception of having to hunt their own food they were no different than the lions walking around eating gazelles in Africa. These big cats were as wild as my aunt Nancy when the fleet came to shore. She was a big Ole girl, her feet were all beat out like canoe paddles but that's a story for a different book.

Anyway, an announcement was made for all animal people to report to the set. Being called an animal person is the same as being called a soundman and I know how we all love being known as our craft instead of our names. Besides people that really know me would never call me sound. I was excited to be on my first film set. I walked out there and Noel said stand right here. All the animal handlers and most of the crew got in two lines, facing each other about 4 to 5 feet apart. For the life of me I could not figure out what we were doing so, I thought it must be some kind of film thing. The 2 lines of people went from the animal compound to this house that they had built on the edge of a lake as part of the set. Courtney Goodin who was next to me in line was the sound mixer on the show. He ended up being a good friend. I turned and asked him what is going on. Before he could answer there was a sound kind of like a combination of panic and thunder, but then I saw it. 40 of these untrained basically wild lions, tigers, cougars, and leopards started running down this human chute we had created. This crazy man Noel, was chasing them with a large piece of plywood yelling and screaming shaking a four by eight piece of plywood as he ran after them. My first thought was run and don't look like a gazelle. Then I hear Noel yelling do not run or they will get you. My second thought was just because I worked at the St. Louis Zoo, I am not Marlin Perkins and how the hell did I end up on wild kingdom. As the cats (the smallest one weighing in at about 85lbs and the biggest at about 500 lbs) would run and walk by they would bump into you. They then would look at you like you were a soup bone. I ask Courtney if this was a common thing and do you guys do this sort of thing a lot? He looked at me and said you are not going to like the answer. This turned out to be one of the saner things they did on that film and to this day I am surprised no one died.

Over the course of a year I watched several people get bit and sent to the hospital. I also watched Noel get bit more than anybody else and HE WAS IN CHARGE!!!!! I helped pull a tiger off of Jan Debont and he ended up having 500 stitches in his head. Why didn't I quit? It's like the old joke about the guy who cleans up after the elephant someone asks him why he doesn't get a better job his answer is "and what give up show business?".

During this film Courtney's boom man Larry Abramson did leave the film. Gee I don't know why! Just because while trying to do sound work you were dodging big cats. Some of the cats were on the rafters above you, some on railings next to you and some walking over your feet as you tried to move to boom an actor. I had been hanging with Courtney and basically he took me under his wing and taught me booming. I had helped engineer records I had played on and knew something about sound. I trained animals so Courtney figured I would fit in. I was used to being around exotic animals that could kill you or make you walk and talk funny for the rest of your life, but I was used to trained animals not these. These filmmakers really had nerves to put up with this. There were only 3 real animal trainers on the film. Myself and 2 other guys, the rest were people hired off the street to throw meat and be human shields. There was a flood and a major fire that swept through the compound during the course of the film. Several people, including Courtney were stuck on what became a very small island. They had to be winched across a raging river in a harness, in the dark, as things like houses, cars, propane tanks, kem editing machines, and trucks were whizzing by them in the water. A wall of water mowed down all the cages.

With no electricity and in the pitch black all you could see all around you were pairs of green eyes from the 100 or so big cats staring at you. It took almost 30 hours to catch all the cats that were running lose everywhere. Then there was a fire that swept through the canyon and I had to walk the very nervous elephants down the road with a police escort to safety. Here I thought filmmaking was going to be exciting, little did I know. All of this was written in Tippis book "The cats of Shambala".

After that I tried to get to know everybody that had anything to do with the business. I even hung out at Audio Services which has since changed their name to Location Sound services. This company caters to sound professionals all over the world and my good friend David Panfilli still runs the business. Finally I went to Universal and drove them crazy. I really did not know anything except how to kind of boom. I had only done one show and on that one I was standing in a room with 10 to 20 big cats while trying to boom actors. Needless to say, I was always watching the cats rather than the actors. There was a woman we called the black widow. She had had a gaggle of husbands who died. She did all the highering at Universal for the sound dept. Her real name was Janet and she ended up liking me, which was as important back then as it is today. She couldn't hire me at first because I wasn't in the union. If you did not have a relative in the business it was impossible to get in and the elephants did not count. I was only short a couple of days and I was very persistent. She eventually had me loading dummies and working in the shop until I got the rest of my days I needed. At the same time I was spending everyday on a Fisher boom, learning how to use it. I would go down to the stages and learn about lenses and lighting. I finally got my days in and now she was assigning me to shows as a boom man.

That's the way it was done in those days. You did not have to look for work it was assigned to you when you worked for a studio. At Universal we had to park way in the back off of Barham Boulevard and take a shuttle to the department you worked in to punch a time card. I would get off at the corner and walk to the sound department to punch my time card. It did not matter what you did everybody punched a time card. As I walked to the department this black Lincoln would pass me every morning. This went on for about a year.

One morning I was either late or the Lincoln was early and as I walked by Alfred Hitchcock got out of the Lincoln. He saw me and said, "You with the red hair come here." I walked over to him and he asked me "where are you going?" I told him I was going to the sound department to punch my card. He told me that he had seen me every morning for about a year and was just curious. Then he stuck out his hand and said I'm Alfred Hitchcock. I shook his hand and said I know who you are I'm Tim Cooney. After that day every time Alfred Hitchcock would see me he would wave to me. He died not to long after that but I will always have that fond memory of our short talk and the times he waved at me. I heard he left that Lincoln to the driver that was with him all those years.

I ended up booming such shows as Buck Rodgers in the 23-century, Battle Star Galactica the original with Lorne Green, The Incredible Hulk, Night Rider, The Incredible Shrinking Woman, Quincy, and many others. Back in the 70s you never worked past midnight. You got night premium after eight pm and if you did work past midnight it was double whatever your rate was at the time. It was just too expensive to work late and we actually could spend time at home with our families. We obviously have given up too much and in return it seems all we got was the right to keep working.

This is the way I got into the business. I think with the exception of the guys who had relatives in the business most of the guys like me kind of fell into it. I am starting my 35th year making movies and television shows. I still play music with whom ever will let me because I love it. For me it has been a rewarding career with enough diverse situations to keep me from being bored. Before I finish this chapter I want to tell you a story. It's about Catering on the shows. It's the only time in the book I talk about them and they are so important. For the most part they are pretty good and Tony's Food Catering is the best in my opinion. John Travolta has Tony's in his contract and if you ever have him on a show you will know why. Then there are the others. They should figure out that the round thing in the truck is a smoke alarm and not a timer. They don't need to wait for that sucker to go off before the food is done. In our business we have to eat catered food more than home cooked meals and for the most part they are painfully adequate.

Anyway back in the 70s and 80s you would walk out of the stage around 7pm and could hear the stripper steaks hit the grill, all over the back lot. At Universal it was always Michelson's catering. One time I did this independent film and the catering company was called Dee-lite catering. Trust me when I tell you they were not. I grabbed a plate of food and everybody was complaining how bad the food was and that it tasted funny. When I sat down to try to eat it I couldn't. I really could not eat it. I did not even recognize it. The caterer was set up on a street in the valley and there were 2 dogs running around hoping for a free meal. So I set my plate on the ground. One of the dogs sniffed at it and took one bite went and laid down and do what dogs do, started licking himself. One of the cooks came out of the truck and said "what is that dog doing?" I told him "I think he's trying to get the taste out of his mouth." Everybody had a good laugh many people got sick and we had a different caterer the next day.

Thanks to motion picture catering I am now on a diet. I am trying to get back to my original weight of 7 pounds 8 ounces. To sum it all up If you follow what you read in this book and act on it you will have a career in the business. All you have to figure out now is if this is really what you want to do.

Chapter 3

ACTING AND BACKGROUND

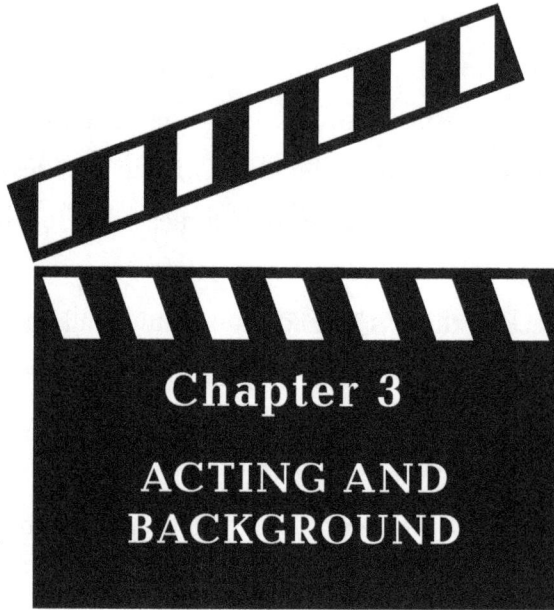

The reason I have lumped extras and serious acting in the same chapter is to be a good extra, you have to know something about acting and every extra I ever met said they were an actor. Now let us cut to the chase. Never work as an extra if you want to be a serious actor. If you just want to make a few bucks sign up with every extra casting company in town. When you do never pay more than fifteen dollars to register. Most of them advertise in Variety Backstage west and the Hollywood reporter. At the very least you will learn what happens on the set. Then if you decide you want to get into the business seriously, you will have a better idea of what you really want to do. By the way, working as an extra is not considered serious. Extras make minimum wage and a free meal. Many people do it as a whim. When the extras had their own union it was different. There were professional extras. They knew how to make it look real. The extras would wear rubber sole shoes so as not to ruin the sound tracks. Professional extras knew when to stay in the light and when to stay out. They would hit specific marks or do a specific piece of business. But since their union folded anybody can be an extra and for minimum wage you don't exactly get the cream of the crop. Now the extras that are union are under the SAG or AFTRA contract. Should you be lucky enough to look like a particular actor, you could get a job as a stand-in. A stand-ins job is to watch every rehearsal and stand in the same places the actor did. After the rehearsal the actor will go to wardrobe and make-up and the stand in will go through the actors motions so the crew can light the set. Stand ins make about a hundred and twenty dollars for eight hours and get a little more respect than an extra mostly because they are there everyday with the crew. Now to harp on the theme of this book. When you work as an extra, it is important that you cultivate a relationship with the second and first assistant director. They are the ones that will always hire you and they have the power to request you from the agencies you are registered with. If you are a stand in you must cultivate a relationship with the star you are standing in for. On a certain detective show in Hawaii, there was a stand in who would set up a table next to this actor's chair. He would then put coffee or tea the actor's favorite brand of cigarettes and whatever else the actor wanted. Everybody would tease him, but he stayed employed for the entire run of the show. I heard he did other shows with that actor after the series folded. So it just depends how badly you want to work in this business. Some people would say that waiting on this actor was demeaning, but this stand in saw it as an opportunity. The outcome is as a stand in you might get one line of dialog if you are lucky, but you will never be taken serious as an actor. So if you want to be an extra work part time or full time with the stars. It is the easiest job to get. Now the extras work under the screen actor's guild contract so they have a union again (kind of). Just call the Screen Actor's Guild or AFTRA for the details.

Serious acting is probably the hardest single career in the film business. Acting seems to be the most sought after job in the business. For every one acting job, there are at least two hundred actors who could do the job. There are at least one hundred actors who could do the job well. There are at least twenty-five actors who could do the job great! The trick in becoming a working actor is two fold. Should you be lucky enough to have a relationship with a star on his word alone, you could get a minor role on a big picture. The same is true if you have that kind of a relationship with a director. That is why you see Clint Howard in most of Ron Howard's films. Clint is Ron's brother. That is just one example. If you look at other films you will see the same actors working with say Clint Eastwood, Sly Stallone, and others. But if you are like most of the wanna be actors you will have to attack! When I say attack, I mean you will have to be more aggressive than you ever have in your life. You will have to give new meaning to the word networking. Your set of goals should be the following. One get a S.A.G. card, two get an agent, three work, work, work. There are several ways to get a S.A.G. card and I won't go into that in detail here. Call the guild for that information.

First if you don't have any experience, get some. These are my suggestions. The best thing to do first is to take some classes. You are better off with a well-known acting coach. Sometimes when you go in for a reading to get a part they will ask you who you have studied with. It always sounds better if you are studying with someone the directors and producers know. Should the part come down between you and one other person just the fact that you are studying with someone they know will give you the edge. Many actors such as Nina Foch, Clu Gallager, Jeff Goldblum, and others run workshops and classes. I don't know what the cost is and in some cases you might have to audition just to get into the class. This of course is the first good step in building a relationship with a person who could help you out later. If you can't afford or get into one of those classes check out your local college. Don't pay for classes from some unknown. If you can't get into a class with a well known, you are better off saving your money and getting some experience from your local college. There are so many con men out there running so-called schools. One of their ploys is to have a showcase at the end of the semester where supposedly agents will come and watch you perform. Then by the time you drive home from the performance there is a message on your machine. The message says "we are not asking everybody back but you were exceptional and we are extending an invitation to you to continue in our school." Of course you are not experienced enough to know if you were good or not so your ego gets you sucked in and your money with it.

Practice, practice, practice! Run lines and rehearse various parts with anybody who will listen to you. Everybody will have an opinion take it with a grain of salt. Keep in mind the only person you have to impress is the one who is going to hire you. The more you practice, the more confidence you will have when you have to read for a part. This will also help get rid of your inhibitions which is necessary to be a good actor. So many times a script will have silly dialog, but someone without inhibitions who is a decent actor can pull it off.

There are classes in nothing but cold readings. A cold reading is where you go in for a job and they ask you to read the part. You have no time to study the part, but you must make it believable on the spot. Shelly Winters who of course is an established actress went in for a part. The director and producer told her they had written the part for her and she was perfect and they had no one else in mind for the part. Then they asked her if she could just read a couple of lines. Without getting out of her chair she reached down and she opened up her bag and pulled out her Oscar and set it on the desk. She said something like "some people seem to think I know how to act I don't read for parts ". She refused to read. She left the office and got the part anyway. The picture was the Poseidon Adventure. The point is cold readings are the hardest thing to do because you never really know what they want in the way of an actor. It is obvious they thought she was right for the part and had her in mind all the time. I wonder how many other actresses read for the part and thought they had a chance? Because you don't know what the producer and director are looking for it is kind of a crapshoot. Even actors who have been in the business for years hate to read for a part. So the best preparation is to read parts out loud with friends, so that you become accustomed to hearing your own voice. When you practice your parts you must do some research. You must become that character! On the film Scarface, Al Pachino was always in character. While the crew was preparing for the next shot Al would walk around and talk to people with the accent and hold a conversation with you as the character he was playing in the film. That is a form of method acting and Lee Strassberg became famous for teaching it. Then there is the other side of the coin. On the film Marathon Man, Dustin Hoffman stayed up all night to get into character for the next days work. When he came in the next morning Sir Lawrence Oliver asked Dustin what had happened to him because he looked so awful. Dustin told him that he had stayed up all night to prepare his character. Dustin then asked him how he prepared for his character. Sir Lawrence then said "easy I am an actor so I act." This was Sir Lawrence way of saying he did not believe in method acting and was quite a great put down to Dustin. So when you start studying you will learn the various forms of acting. Hopefully you will find some sort of method that works for you.

You should always read Backstage West and the trades because they always list casting calls both S.A.G and non-S.A.G talent. When you are first starting your career, go after every job. Stage plays are good because you will learn how to deal with a live audience and get a good sense of timing. You will also get immediate feedback of your talents. Also there doesn't seem to be as much competition for those jobs. At least then when you go up for part in a film or televisions show you will have some credits. The more interviews you go to the better odds you will have of landing the job. Also if you do enough cold readings you will get more relaxed and comfortable with them. You should do something towards your career every day. You should call casting directors set up interviews and even on Sunday do something towards building your career.

On Sundays you could read the trades and decide what jobs to go for on Monday. Maybe you go to a club where agents are looking for new talent.

The important thing is to get noticed by people who can help your career any way you can. I heard a story and I know it's true, Because Kris told me it was. Kris Kristofferson had given himself a certain amount of time to sell his songs in Nashville or he was going to go into another line of work. He had made a deal with his parents. He was fast approaching his time with very little success. At the time like so many of us in the 60s we did what we had to do not to go to Vietnam. So he was flying helicopters for the National Guard on the weekends. Mostly out of frustration and his desire to become a success One Sunday morning he landed a helicopter on Johnny Cashes back lawn. John came out to see what was happening. Kris gave him his tapes and told him he needed a break. John got him his first deal. He went the full distance to get him to listen to his songs, the rest is history. The point of the story is that he got noticed and he had talent. He made his own luck. Without getting noticed his talent may never have gotten a chance to be used. So do what you have to do to get noticed? That's a question only you can answer. So do something everyday to further your career and get noticed.

Chapter 4

Production Producers and Directing

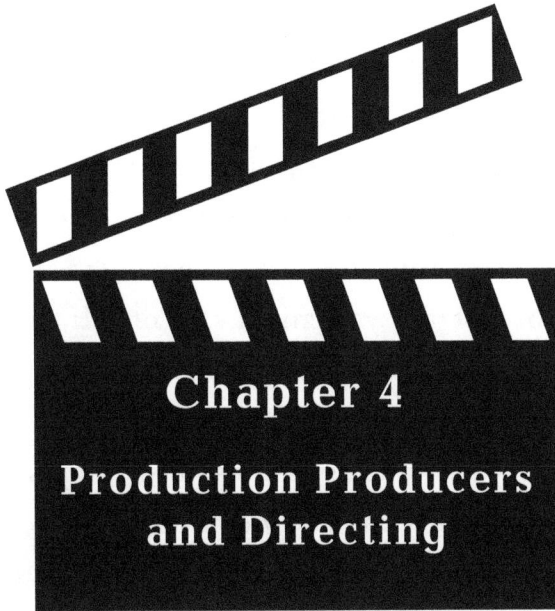

The reason I have put directing and production in the same chapter is because so many producers direct and so many directors produce. Production involves many people. Starting with secretary's, production coordinator's, production assistant's, unit production manager's, assistant to producers, assistant directors, associate producers', producers, executive producers and on television, show runners. We will touch briefly on what each does, but what is more important we will tell you how to get those positions.

Secretaries are the lifeblood of any production company and I know a few who went on to produce their own films and run other production companies. I will call them secretaries, which is what they are at the studios but coordinators on the films themselves. Secretaries might sound demeaning, but once you know all the things that they do they should really be called problem solvers. It's just many of the jobs are interchangeable. As a secretary in this business your most important job will be to field calls coordinate many things and lie a lot. For instance if your boss doesn't want to talk to someone, they are always in a meeting. For instance you might say "oh Mr. Cooney is not available, he is in a meeting with some financial people at the moment." This really means Mr. Cooney ran to the ATM. Some other typical lies are. "The position is filled and yes we will start on time" and of course my all time favorite, "we can't pay you your usual rate". If you are a secretary or an executive assistant, keep hounding the major studios until you get in the secretarial pool. Find out about upcoming shows either through Backstage West Variety, The Hollywood Reporter, Production Weekly, or Production Alert. In my case I get them all. Do a search online for these publications. They will tell you every show that is getting ready to start. When you find a job opening don't call, go there in person and remember everybody's name. If you need the address of the office where they would hire you call and tell them you need to send a package and they will give you the address. Then go there beg, bribe, do whatever it takes to get the gig. Then work your ass off. I have helped people in the past and told them I can get you the job, but I can't keep it for you. If you get lucky enough to end up at a studio you will bounce around to many different offices until you are permanently assigned. After that put into practice what I said in the introduction of this book. If you feel lucky maybe you will meet another secretary who gets a job and recommends you. Maybe you meet a producer who will hire you. Some producer likes you and has a relationship with Brad Pitt. All of a sudden you have a certain limited access. Word of mouth is everything. Eventually you do enough shows to move up to production coordinator, which is a short cut to producing. Also become computer smart with the programs they use in the film business. I know someone who got a job because she knew how to work with "movie magic" and now she produces films. Be sure to read the trades and every source for upcoming films and projects so you can offer your services.

Associate producers are nothing more than glorified producer assistants. After you have assisted a producer for a while and they think you are competent, they give you the title of associate producer. It's cheaper than a raise. You will definitely have to ask or beg for the title, but it is important so you can begin your crawl upwards in the business. The upside is that you are able to develop relationships with box office names. Once you have developed these relationships with stars, producers, and writers you can think about putting a project together. A very smart lady was an associate producer for one of the biggest producers in Hollywood. She parlayed that and her relationships into running Demi Moores company. Her sister was Bruce Willis's assistant. Later her sister and herself started their own company and produced a film staring Mike Meyers. The film was Austin Powers. They are respected because they started at the bottom worked hard and ended up being a success.

Like I said earlier on all you need now is a great script, a box office name, and you can go to one of your many contacts at the studio and make a deal. Just advance to go and collect a little more than two hundred dollars.

Production assistants are entry-level employees. (The bottom feeders of the production world.) This is where you will have to start if you don't have any relatives or good friends in the business. Maybe you can't get into one of the directing programs, so this is the way you will have to do it.

P.A.s as they are called do everything from running errands to sometimes filling in for background on some shows. Your first job is critical and now I am going to tell you something I am going to repeat a few more times in this book. FIRST JOB WORK FOR FREE! Yes, that's what I said free. To get your foot in the door pick a great project with a well-known director. Pick a bad project with a well-known director (there are plenty of them) and offer to work on the project for free. A show will only last about 3 months or less and you will have a good credit. To find a good project read Daily Variety or The Hollywood Reporter they always list upcoming projects and who's directing them. There is also a publication called National Film Sources out of Scranton PA. That costs under $100 a year. It lists all future projects. I have mentioned others. Once you pick a project simply march into the production office (DO NOT CALL) and tell the secretary you want to work as a P.A on their current film. You are willing to work for free or next too free (they might pay you something for insurance purposes) so that you will have a good credit to start your career. At the very least get the production managers and the A.D's names and try to make contact with those people. It is usually the first or second A.D that hires the P.As. After you accomplish that and you will, if you perservere. While you are still working start to find your next job. You will hear about other upcoming shows while you are still on your current one. It always sounds better when you walk into a production office and say "I am just finishing up on a film for Steven Spielberg and was wondering if you have hired your P.As yet?" At least on your next job you won't have to work for free. Before you leave your first job try to get the producer or AD or who ever you are working for to give you a letter of recommendation, since you won't have much of a resume. It might be difficult to get a good P.A job, but try to stay away from the B movies. You will have an easier time getting your next job if you have just finished working as a P.A on Jurassic Park, as opposed to Teenage Hitchhiking Sleez Bitches From Outer Space.

The next logical step is assistant director. After you have had a job as a P.A. you will see what a first and second assistant director does. Once you are familiar with those responsibilities you will want to move up as soon as possible because P.As make minimum wage with no benefits. Read the chapter on union verses non-union in the book.

At this point you have three ways to go. One if a production company loves you and they have enough pull they can go to the D.G.A (Directors Guild of America). They can talk to them about you working as a second, second on their projects but you must have enough hours as a PA. There are some restrictions such as you can only work as a second for that particular production company. If they don't have any projects coming up you will be back to square one but with credits. There are other restrictions but eventually you get your required days and then you can work for anybody that will hire you. Two if you have a degree you can apply for the D.G.A training program. The program is excellent and if you get in you get to skip the whole P.A part of the procedure. The D.G.A will put you on several shows and move you around for the length of the program and then after that you are on your own. At the end of the program you are a second assistant director and registered that way with the guild. During your time on the program you have met many first and second A.Ds. When you are finished with the program hopefully one of them loved you as a trainee and will hire you now that you are a second or a second, second. Three (and the least desirable) try to get a job as a second, second on a low budget non-union film. If they hire you it will strictly be budgetary and you won't sleep much. You will get some good experience and learn a lot. The disadvantage is that like I have said before whatever circle you start to run in that is where you will stay for a while. Always try for the better projects even if they are low budget. Always save your crew sheets and check stubs because they will help prove your days to the guild when you try to join. I don't write down what the requirements are for the guild because they do change regularly and you can find out with a phone call. Working as a second on non-union films will get you into the guild with the required days.

Once you are in the guild work only union. I know people who started as a PA. worked as a second finally got their days joined the guild and never worked a union job. They became first A.Ds production managers and even directed and never got out of that circle. The object of the game is to move up. Okay so to sum it all up, my recommendation is to try to get in to the D.G.A program. Their program is called the trainee program it is practically impossible to get in, but it is kind of like winning the lotto except every year there are only twenty to thirty winners. Disney has their own program and there is a company called Chanticleer films that has a program. These are the best. All of them are almost impossible, but then you picked this business. See you should have listened to your mother and you would have had your own church or synagogue by now. To become a first assistant director you must have a certain number of days as a second and what is more important someone who will hire you as a first.

The first A.D. as he is called runs the set. There is a saying in the business "it is the directors movie but the first A.D.s set". The first A.D. sets up the board. The board used to be a heavy cardboard affair that folds up like an accordion. Inside are cardboard strips that have every scene you are going to shoot. Now the board is all done on the computer. As a rule the first will consult with the U.P.M producer and director when he is setting up the board. Many factors will determine in what order you will shoot the project, the actor's availability, location availability, whether the director wants to get up that early, you know the important things. Basically you have to set up a schedule that will work into the time frame and budget and still make everybody happy. You really can't be a unit production manager (U.P.M) without having worked as an assistant director or some kind of production secretary or coordinator.

A U.P.M hires most of the crew, works out the deals with crew members, and lives or dies by his budget. If the picture goes along fine the producer is the hero he will probably hire you again because every producer knows the value of a good U.P.M. If the picture is over budget, not on schedule the U.P.M is the whipping post and it might be hard to get your next job. Hollywood is a small town and everybody hears about everybody's success or failures. Regardless how bad it might be all is eventually forgotten and you will work again. The saying is "you will never work in this town again until they need you." You can't be a good producer without understanding this job. You can't do the job until you understand it.

So how do you become a U.P.M? The best way is to be a good first A.D. Work for the same companies that like your work so they will have faith in you to move you up. Another way is if you are a good secretary or production coordinator a U.P.M may have enough faith in you to become a production coordinator. As a production coordinator you then learn what a U.P.M does how to make the deals and work out contracts. I am not just talking actors contracts (which you probably won't deal with) but, contracts with crew, contracts for locations and other things, which as the U.P.M you have to approve. The advantages of being a U.P.M are you can do many other production related jobs. I know U.P.Ms that bounce between being an A.D and producer. I know some vice presidents at major studios that got those jobs being good U.P.Ms. Also many U.P.Ms also get line producer credits. Notice I said a good producer. There are many producers who were never U.P.M s. Their daddy owns the studio or at least is in charge. Possibly they play golf in the right circles and are hired as an associate producer until they learn the ropes.

I worked on a television show where the stars son, who just got out of rehab, was put to work as a dialog coach. The next year he directed a few episodes (everybody helped him). At the end of the next season, the star changed the entire crew (all the people that helped the son). He of course stayed there and ended up directing every other episode. When the show went off the air he never directed anything his mother was not in. My point is that the more powerful your friends are the less competent you have to be. I saw one of the people who had done that show, he had a t-shirt on that said "mommy mommy help me". He told me he had been fired for wearing the shirt. The lesson here is that even some of the most powerful people in the business can feel threatened by one of their low level employees. Especially if there job has been handed to them and they are not qualified for it. Also that falls into the don't piss anyone off category. Since then the actress has retired and the son has not directed since. But then he could not direct traffic to begin with let alone a film or TV show. He made millions and his mom was worth millions so he never has to work anyway. So it goes back to what I have said make lots of friends no enemies and become competent at whatever job you decide to do. Those two things are a powerful combination in today's film business.

Let's talk about directing. In order for you to be a good director you must know how to edit. What little pieces of film you must shoot to have a good flow from scene to scene. So you can manipulate your audience. My personal feeling is if you manipulate your audience subtly it is better. In my opinion Steven Spielberg manipulates his audiences with a sledgehammer and he is considered a great director, so it is just a matter of taste. I prefer a director that lets the audience make up there own mind instead of being pushed into a point of view. If it is possible to get your hands on a video camera write and direct a five or ten minute short. It really doesn't matter what it is about but you will learn what is involved.

Get a computer program and put it together just so long as you learn how to edit. They now have some great programs on the computer to edit so it has become a lot easier to teach yourself. Then you will learn about angles and how to manipulate the audience to your way of thinking. You will see that if you had shot this close up differently it would have been better or more dramatic or possibly you could have used a different cut. Once you start doing it you will see what I mean. If there is anyway you can get an opportunity to spend some time with a professional editor do it. Even if you work for him for free.

If you are one of the lucky few that can write a script it is the best way to become a director. Many directors started off as either writers or editors. The studio always feels more comfortable when the director has had a lot of input into the script. Let's say you have a script an your agent is trying to sell it. One of the conditions could attach you to the deal as the director. This would only happen if it were a low budget film or after you have had several scripts that were a success.

So here is the summary of what to do if you do secretarial work. If you are a secretary and want work in production learn the programs (such as final draft movie magic there are many ect.ect.)

2. Call production companies to find out there address go there and offer your services.

3. Try the major studios until you get in.

4. Develop a relationship so you will end up working for the same producer for a while.

5. Develop as many relationships as you can.

WORK IN MOVIES? ARE YOU CRAZY?   33

So here is the summary of what to do for P.A work.

1. Be willing to work for free on your first job. Find out who the production manager, assistant directors are and talk to them about your services.

3. Make sure to get a letter of recommendation before the project is over to use to get your next gig.

4. Try to line up your next job while you are still working.

So here is the summary of what to do for A.D work.

1. Check out and try to get into one of the programs.

2. Check with the D.G.A get the latest requirements and work as a P.A to get the days you need.

3. If you have to work on lower budget projects to get your days do it but only for the experience and your days.

To become a production coordinator or upm do all of the above and hope you have the right timing and luck.

To become a director

1. Write everyday until you have a script that sells
2. Learn camera angles editing and story telling to manipulate the audience
3. RELATIONSHIPS

Producers

1. Get a job working for a producer and develop relationships
2. Write scripts get an agent to represent your scripts. This is easier to do if you are already working for a producer. Maybe with luck and a relationship some box office actor will like it.
3. If you know money people try to get investors to fund your script.

So go for it catch the brass ring win the lottery but most importantly find something you like doing and do it. You might find out that after a while you like something else in the business. I know many people that started out as actors and ended up in production. They worked more and were a bigger success.

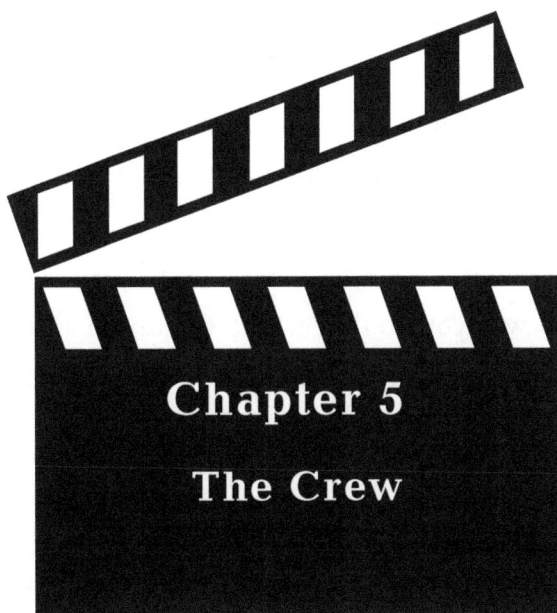

Chapter 5

The Crew

This section of the book will deal with the technical side of the business. This covers camera, sound, makeup, hair, wardrobe, special effects, grip, electric, greens, construction, painters, craft service, and even animals. These are the people that work the hardest and are responsible for the end product. Without these craftsmen the project could never be made. Each department has there own union and local but all with the exception of drivers and animal trainers are members of the IA. IA is short for The International Alliance Of Theatrical Stage Employees. You must be a member of this union to work in the film business. It does not matter if it is television or movies you have to be a member.

My recommendation is before you pursue your career it would be good to have a years worth of cash in the bank. The other option is if you have a husband, wife, girlfriend, sugar daddy, anybody, that will help pay the bills, that's important. Why? Because you need to put all your effort and time into your career. This is the only way to succeed. You must do something everyday to further your career even on Sunday until your established. For years the only way you could get into the union and business was to have a relative get you in. Then you would learn the job at the studio you worked at. Those days are gone now you must learn the job on the job or go to a film school where you will learn the basics.

One way, of getting into one of these crafts and getting a union card is getting a job at a related business. As an example if you want to get into the lighting department go to the rental houses that supply lights for film and television. Get a job there. Drive them crazy until they hire you. Go see them everyday. You will meet many lighting guys you will learn all the terms used in the business as well as the different kinds of lights and cables you will work with. If that lighting company is union and you work for them for thirty consecutive days you will automatically get into the union. Should you want to get into sound try to get a job at a transfer house or at a place where they rent sound gear to the industry. Make sure it's a union house. The same holds true for any craft that uses specific gear that has to be rented. Which is most of them.

The makeup department is a little different. You have to have those skills going in. The Westmores (who are a Hollywood icon when it comes to makeup) have a school, which I hear is excellent.

There are others as well but be careful because there are many rip offs. I would call the makeup local and see whom they might recommend at least you know that school would be legitimate. The school will tell you the ins and outs of the makeup part of the industry and you will make future contacts, which are important to your success in the business.

As I have tried to emphasize in this book, try to make contacts while you are working at these related jobs. If you are working at Panavision (the camera rental house) try to get to know the many assistants and operators that come in to prep their shows. Let them know that you are interested in working in production. Push gently until one of them gives you a chance. Find out where they are shooting and ask if you can hang out and help. After you hang out for a while you will get a feel for the job. The same applies to all of the other related jobs. Like I have said before if you can afford it, work your first job for free. Very few people will turn you down knowing they are going to get extra help and it won't cost them anything. If you help out for free and do the job well next time maybe they will hire you or at least recommend you to someone. Also you will have a legitimate film on your resume.

I know a guy who wanted to move from cable man to boom man on the sound crew so he took a very difficult show in Alaska in the wintertime. The sound mixer couldn't find any other boom man to do it so he took this cable man. It just so happens that this guy turned out to be a great boom man and now he makes good money and is more sought after more than the boom man that turned the Alaska show down. Sometimes you make your own luck and opportunities.

Like other businesses the film community is very clannish. Film people like to talk shop.

So the sooner you establish yourself the better your chances will be. The friendships you make will last a lifetime. Angela Landsbury once told me a great story that will illustrate my point. Although she was just a little older than Elvis Presley, she had played his mother in the film "Blue Hawaii". For many years after that Elvis had always sent her a card or something for mothers day. This went on for years. That not only shows you what kind of person Elvis was, but also the relationship that was established in a short time making a film. I also think of it as a great tribute to Angela Landsbury, who made the role so believable that it apparently impressed even Elvis, who had very deep feelings for his mother.

Okay, so maybe you don't want to work in a related business. The next best thing is to find out about jobs by reading the trades and talking to people. Approach the company about working as an intern for little or no money. Make sure that at the end of the show you get a letter of recommendation so that even though you won't have much of a resume you will have something.

Let's talk a minute about lying on your resume. I have never lied on mine but I have exaggerated. Here's the example. When I went from TV to films I took a lot of second unit work. Actually I took any work I could get as long it was a film. Second unit is when the picture usually has been wrapped they have edited the picture and they need extra scenes. So they try to get the original people but in my case the original guys were already on a different picture. So on my one page resume I would put the name of the picture and the fact that I mixed the sound. When I was asked I always told them I was the second unit mixer. But they had to ask. I know some people when they start out they put down they have done commercials because commercial companies come and go and it's impossible to verify the information. If you do that make sure you know how to handle yourself on the set and do your job. When you do get a gig try to make friends with the people you are working with. Remember everybody's name. Then on their next show you will go with them. Also, while you are working keep your ears open because everybody will be talking about their next project.

That of course is what it is all about, finding your next job. I know people in this business that have won Oscars and Emmys they don't hustle their next job and they sit at home wondering why they are not working. Ten years ago if you had won an award it would help you land a job. Today the most it does is get you the interview. The same doesn't apply to actors but it is true of the crafts. What will eventually happen is you will establish relationships with the people you work for. Then they will hire you over and over. Unfortunately when the people you know don't have a show it can be difficult to establish new contacts for a job. In most cases you will establish a new contact only if their regular people are not available. Then try to impress the people you are working for so you can ace out the old competition next time.

Let's talk about timing. Timing is very important because if you contact a company and they are not hiring yet you have wasted their time and yours. Sometimes you will alienate those people because they have other things going on and they are not ready to talk about your position. So always find out when they plan to hire your particular position. If you are not the head of a department, find out who is so you can approach that person for a job. As a rule the U.P.M will hire the head of the department and the head of the department will have his people. The head of the department also has the authority to hire more people if his regular people are not available. So if you are a make-up person or hair person the trick is to get to know head make-up and hair people so they will hire you.

I was just finishing up Die Hard two and really needed a vacation because that show was so difficult. I just happen to hear about this show for Disney even though it was for one of their other companies called Hollywood Pictures. Anyway, on a whim I called to see if I could get an interview. I did not know anybody so I figured it would not happen. As it turned out I got the interview and the job. That was timing. That was from a cold call, because like I said I did not know anybody connected with the show. The picture was called the "Marrying Man" staring Alec Baldwin and Kim Bassinger. That was the picture they met on and seduced each other. They were constantly fighting with the studio. Kim and Alec ended up getting married later divorced and left me with some great stories. For me to have gotten a major picture from a cold call almost never happens anymore.

On a film and many television shows it goes like this. First a director almost always gets the people he wants. On television it's the show runner. The exception to the rule is a new director working with seasoned producers. Unless the director is very adamant about a person or a department he will be so busy and inexperienced he wont want to deal with crew. So the order is Director or show runner, producers, UPM, production coordinator, then after that maybe somebody on the show might recommend you to a producer or somebody. So you see a cold call is a long shot. I still send my resume out all the time to the productions just because my name is read and forgotten about. But then later when someone is looking for a sound mixer and my name is brought up they have heard of me. They won't remember from where but they know they have heard of me. This has worked for me on more than one occasion. So now you know who you have to get to know and impress if you want to stay employed. If you want to impress do the best job you can and do it as low profile as possible. The best compliment I ever got was after a month of shooting. A director came up to me and said we were talking in dallies yesterday and said it really sounded good but know one could remember ever talking to anybody from the sound crew. They did not even know the names of the boom man or cable man and the only reason they knew mine was because they remember me from the interview.

You will end up meeting many people most will end up coleegs a few will end up friends. To finish up this chapter I need to mention this. With the exception of the teamsters your union will not find you work. I have been a member of my union for over thirty years and never once has the union helped me get a job. They have what's called the availability list. When you are out of work you put yourself on that list. Producers who are looking for someone will call the local and get the list or go online to see who is available. I have been told this happens from time to time but I have never gotten a job this way. I have never heard of anyone getting a job this way, but I guess it happens. The teamsters are the only union that still uses the 1 2 3 tier system. As you work longer in the business and have more seniority you move from 3 to 2 then finally 1. All 1s must be hired or at least offered a job before 2s then 3s. Some jobs are so bad 1 and even 2s will turn them down. When it gets busy it happens all the time. So take this information and put it to use. Get a gig maybe it will be the one I am doing.

Chapter 6

Film Schools

Aword about film schools. If you are thinking about going into production or directing then film schools are a good idea. If possible stay with the bigger schools like NYU, USC, or UCLA. There are a few on the east coast and of course AFI. Now there are so many I really don't know which are the good ones. When you walk into a big producers office like Silver Pictures or Steven Spielberg's Amblin Entertainment you tell them that you have your degree. You are interested in working in production. Because you have your degree and maybe went to the same film school someone there did you might get a shot. If you want to work in any other field in the film business decide what you want to do. Once you start working in the business as a grip, boom man, makeup person, ECT. It's very difficult to change careers. Almost impossible. So be sure what you want to do.

Start following the directions in this book and build relationships and your career. I know several associate producers some producers who got their start because they went to the same film school as the producer they were trying to get a job with. Once you learn the basics it is better to get practical experience than spend several years in film school. One way staying in film school could help is if you made a good friend who then went on to get a deal at a studio. Then of course he would hire you. Keep in mind this, the film business pays well, more than what a teacher in film school makes. I think the biggest benefit of film schools are you learn the basics you make relationships that hopefully pay off later and if you write you can bang out some scripts before you graduate and have to make a living. Having scripts that are good and marketable are the high road to producing and directing. The bottom line is if you are not going to direct produce or write you are better off getting a job on a film and starting your career. I have been on many films where there is one P.A with a film degree and One P.A who just hustled the job. You know what? They both make the same amount of money. The film business is not like any other business. Having a degree will not make you any more money. Having a great script will. If you need to go to a good film school to stimulate your creative mind to write that script then go to film school. If you are a self-starter then start.

My elephant training days

clown college graduation 1971

I am back row 5th from the right

The great John McEuen,
Me, Director Randal
Wallace Ibby

Playing music with
the Dillards

Albert lee, me, and Jim

A day of work on We were Soldiers

A day of work in India

David me Chicklis on the Shield

In the studio with John McEuen, me, Rodney Dillard, Ricky Scaggs, Jeff Hanna, and Randy Scruggs

My wife Cherry and Jeff Goldbloom

Me and Cherry and John Amos

Joe Pesci, my daughter Helayna and Danny Glover

Gina Davis and my son Charlie

Brittany Murphy, her husband
Simon, and me

Renee Russo and myself (what a sweetheart!)

Patrick Stewart after *Star Trek*

Playing music with Willie in the bus
(that's one of my guitars!)

A day of golf with Sly

Omar Sharif

King and Queen of Rajihstan

Me & Chris Rock On The Set Of *Lethal Weapon*

Mel Gibson goofin' on me

If you watched *Northern Exposure*, you might recognize Janine Turner (one of my favorites!)

Queen latifa and her dad

Me and Walton on The Shield

CCH Pounder

Chapter 7

Agents

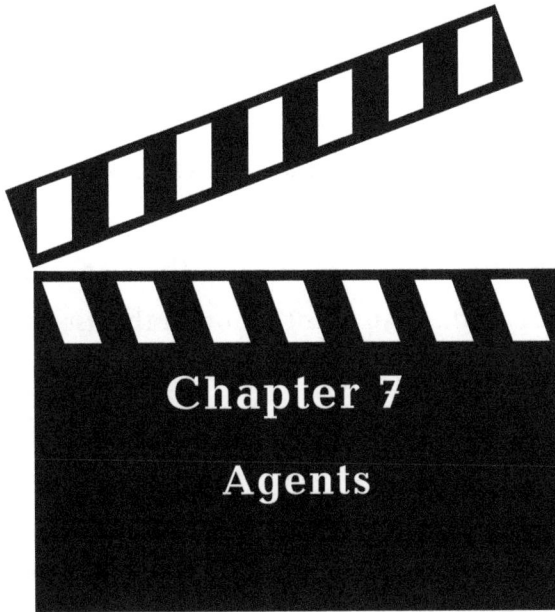

A quick word about agents. If you write direct act and even produce you have to have an agent. The contracts have become so complicated that you have to have an agent to work them out. Many agents out there are actually lawyers. In any of the other fields it is not necessary and you will simply sign a deal memo. The memo will state the terms you have agreed to and is usually a one page affair and pretty simple. How to find and sign an agent is another matter. It is harder to get a good agent than it is to get into one of the unions. Just remember never pay an agent they work strictly on commission and get 10 to 15 percent. An agent that would sign an unknown isn't much of an agent. What usually happens is you get a break and get a job then an agent will sign you. When you are looking for an agent the best timing is if you are working on a low budget film or play and you invite the agent down to see you. Let me expand on that statement. Let's say you are an actor or are trying to be one. Read backstage west. Find a play that is casting and go read for the part. When you finally get a part go to the Screen Actors Guild web Page and print the list of agents. These are the only agents you should deal with. If an agent is not on the list you are wasting your time. Ok so now you are working on a play for no money but it doesn't matter because this job is going to serve a purpose. Go out and buy some postcards or go to a printing shop and have printed on the cards John Doe now appearing in Cats. If your part is one of the main ones you might put that on the card as well. Now you have your cards. Address them to every agent on the list that you downloaded from Screen Actors Guild. Have a rubber stamp made or when they print the cards have them print so it looks like a rubber stamp right across the card in red letters "SEEKING NEW REPRESENTATION" Then put on the card let me know when you are coming so I can comp you at the door. You should get at least 4 to 6 agents to come and see you. The reason is they figure you are already working so you must be able to make money for them. Your first couple of jobs you are going to have to hustle yourself. It is always better to show an agent your talents regardless of the field of work your trying to get into. Always invite more than one agent to see you work on the same night. Most of the agents know each other and when they see their competition interested in you they might sign you very quick. Sometimes if you have a friend that has a good agent they will introduce you to their agent. This is a good way in to an agent that must be good if the friend that introduces you works a lot. If you are working at the time you can say "why don't you come and see me in Cats I can leave your name on the list". If your friend does this consider them a good friend. Most friends won't do this because then you are competition. An agent can be a blessing or a nightmare. Many don't push your career and when you do work take the 10%. The bottom line is having an agent is a very personal situation and a good one will be your friend and mentor and have your career in the front of his mind. I had a great agent, which has just become popular for crew in the last 10 to fifteen years. His name was Darin Sugar and I am mentioning his name in my book because he would have loved it and to me he was the greatest agent in the business. I never knew anyone that loved the business like he did. He worked very hard to become part of the business and he kept my name out there for years. His agency was called Prime Artists and Darin died of a heart attack in his sleep 4 days short of his 43 birthday and I am sure he is up there representing St Peter himself.

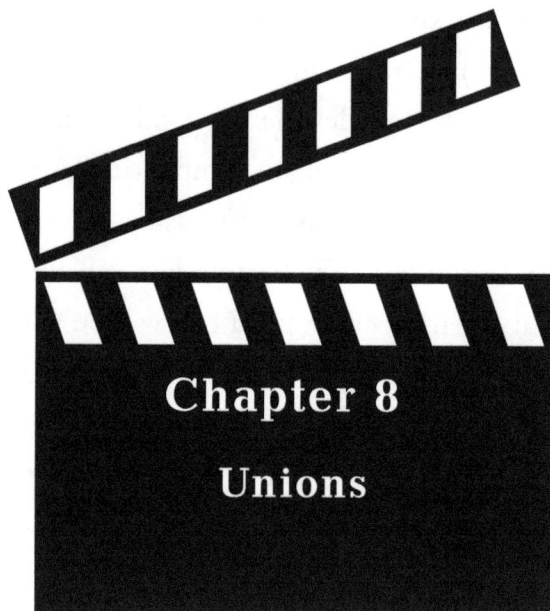

Chapter 8

Unions

Unions should I join? Can they help me? I of course have been a dues paying member for many years. Therefore I am a big supporter of unions. When I got into the business there were few non-union shows and many union shows. Today the opposite is true. Now there are many non-union shows floating around. There are different ways of getting into the union and when the opportunity arises take it. Here is just one example why. In the film business they must feed you or break you to eat every six hours. When they don't they must pay you a meal penalty every half hour until they break. It's not very much I think the first one is $7.50 then it's $10 then the third one is $15. Don't hold me to the exact figures but it is something like that. Over the years I have made thousands of dollars in meal penalties. This is not to say be greedy this is to illustrate a point. Since the producers are willing to pay large sums of money because they don't want to break how often do you think you are going to get a break if they don't have to pay you on a non-union show? This is just one example. When you are on a union show you are guaranteed a certain wage you get medical benefits you get pension benefits so when you retire you have something besides social security. When Ronald Regan was president he did more to hurt the unions than any other president in modern history. He ruined the air traffic controllers union and sent a hard blow to all unions. This from a man who was president of the screen actor's guild. Luckily the anti union attitude is changing. I think that people are starting to realize the unions are just here for protection and hard working family people trying to make a living. Sometimes it is just the greed of the employers that keep them from going union on a show. Sometimes they feel like it's the only way they can complete the project. Even on a low budget show the unions will work with the employer and make concessions so the show can be union. As history shows us we need unions to guarantee a fair wage. It is okay to love your work and want to be involved in films but it is not okay to sell your services cheap. You bring the wage down for everybody else that does your job and contrary to what you might think you will not get any respect from your employer.

The bottom line is why would you want to do the exact same job for less money and no benefits. We work so many hours. I once figured that I work the same amount of hours in seven months, that my friend who has a forty-hour week job does in a year. We are on location away from our families much of the time. We usually end up working in tough locations because visually they are the best for the project. The politics that go with the various positions could be a book in itself. One day you are in a twenty million dollar penthouse and the next day you can't wear a red hat to location because you are shooting in a gang area. Yes the business is diverse enough so that it is interesting. I have been called on the phone at four in the morning because they had to fire a non-union mixer on a show. I had to get on a plane and fly across the entire United States because they thought they could hire cheap labor instead of someone who knows what he is doing. When I have to take my equipment with me that is over twenty cases it is no small challenge. It is also not very cheap. What had happened is that CBS did not like the sound they were getting. So the producers were under the gun to satisfy them. Rather than take another chance they called in a Hollywood professional to save them which is what they should have done in the first place. When I start working on a show you can always tell when someone has been working on non-union films. They have a different attitude and of course they think they are doing it right. In the position I'm in I can sit back and observe. Sometimes the things I see aren't pretty. As long as you learn without the attitude and keep learning you will make it in Hollywood. There is nothing wrong with being non-union to get your start. What I don't like is when people start defending the nonunion way of doing things. All professionals are union and that should be your goal to become a professional.

So how do I get in? There are a couple of ways and I am going to be very general in my terms because every union or guild is different in their requirements. Please don't take these figures exactly because as I write this they are correct but they might change.

First of all if you are on a non-union show and the show goes union while you are shooting you are automatically qualified to join the union. How do you get a non-union show to go union? Very easy. First of all take the non-union show and go to work after day one call the local you intend to join. Tell them you want to organize a show. They will give you a stack of cards. Covertly try to get as many people on the show as possible to sign the cards. Then call the local back. They will approach the producers on the show and inform them the majority of the people on the show have signed a union card and they must go union. It sounds more complicated and scary than it really is. Once you do that everybody on the show is now qualified to join the union. One time I went to Twentieth Century Fox for an interview. I got the job and once I got to location they said the show was non-union. I could not believe it. All the trucks were Fox all the equipment was Fox. So I called the local. The next day there were representatives from several locals there. They told us at lunchtime eat and then don't go back to work. So we sat there for an extra 45 minutes and the show miraculously went union. Everybody on the show was already union anyway. Fox was just trying to do what they do and now that I am getting close to retirement I am glad that show was union. OK so lets take the departments one at a time.

In another chapter I talk about the Directors guild and how to get in but read through these other unions and you will get a better understanding of where we are going in this book.

So if you are an actor and are interested in joining Screen Actors Guild for example call and get the exact requirements. The same goes for all guilds and unions. There are ways of getting in. It used to be you had to have a relative working in the business in order to get in. Then back in the mid seventies they opened up and let people in under certain conditions. As far as SAG in concerned there are two ways of getting in. both difficult. The easiest way to get into SAG is to say one line of dialog on a film or TV show that is signatory with SAG. I have seen it happen. A director sees a background person he likes for some reason usually a pretty girl who has been flirting with the director and gives this person a line of dialog on film. Under the Taft Harley act this person can now join SAG and cannot be turned down. The other way is to work as a background extra and sweet talk an AD to give you a union voucher. Union pays more than non-union and there are rules they have to go by so it's not easy. At the time of this writing when you get three union vouchers you can join SAG. Sign up with a company that hires extras for shows. There are several of them and you won't make anything but minimum wage but if you can get 3 union vouchers you are in. The other way is go on many interviews until you get hired as an actor the minute you are filmed saying a line you are qualified to join.

As far as I know this is the only way to get in. So work work work.

IATSE is the union all of the crafts work under. Camera sound grips lighting makeup hair ect. To get into IATSE you must have thirty consecutive days on a union project. You cannot work on a project unless you are union. Welcome to the wonderful world of the film business. So how do you get around this? As far as I know there are only two ways. First if you have a relationship with someone and they can hire you. Then you can get your days. This can happen as I explain later in the book about working for free. You have worked for free and the person likes you. That person can hire you until the union finds out but hopefully by then you have your 30 days. The key grip is the grip in charge and can hire grips. The gaffer can hire electricians. The sound mixer hires his boom man and cable man ECT. Every department is responsible for hiring their people. If I were you I would start reading the credits at the end of films. Especially in the field of work you are going to pursue. Seek out those people and talk to them. The best way is to call the local union for phone numbers and addresses. Maybe go online to the local page. The sound local for sound guys the grip local for grips ect. They will catch some flack for hiring you but it's not that big of a deal. I have done this for several people. It works well if the show is out of town and you are in another state. The easier way to do it is to start a company. Say you have taken classes and now you are a makeup artist. Call the IA and tell them you want to sell makeup brushes and you want your company to be union. It costs you nothing or very little to have your company signatory. After your company is union hire yourself for at least 30 consecutive days or whatever the requirement is for your local. Make sure you give yourself paychecks that have the days on the stubs and also pay into the pension and health plans. Do everything required by a signatory company. After you have been sworn in to your local shut down the company. Now you are union and anybody can hire you for any union show. This does cost you some money to set everything up and pay into the pension plan but you are investing into your future. If you think being union will help you get work you are wrong. As far as I know only the teamsters local (Drivers) will put you out on a show. For all the rest it's the hustle.

Teamsters can be a difficult union to get into. What I said earlier about relationships hold true here. Once again a pal can really help you out. Here is one trick I know worked. Since all the drivers in the business are teamsters investigate what it would take to become a teamster not related to the film business. I know a guy who drove a tow truck and became a teamster that way. Then all he did was transfer his teamster membership to local 399 in Hollywood. All of the animal trainers in the film business work under the teamster contract unless they do something with their animals on film then they work under the SAG contract. I am a member of IATSE local 695 and the musicians union as well as SAG. I also belong to the Motion Picture Academy the Television Academy and The Cinema Audio Society. All of these are industry related. So now you know how to do it. Do it.

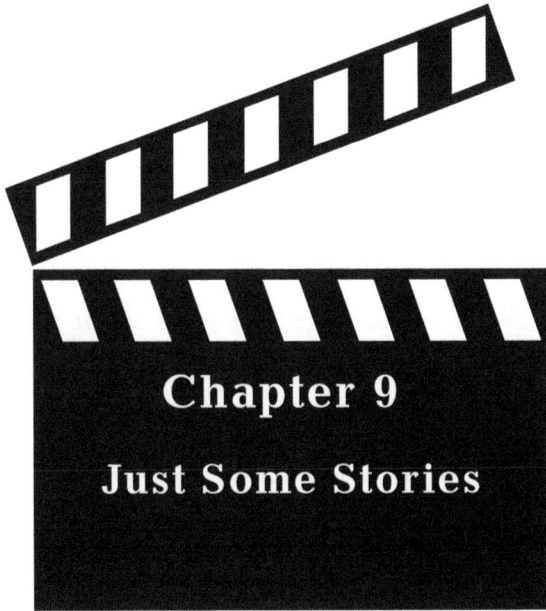

Chapter 9

Just Some Stories

In this chapter are some stories that did not fit anywhere else in the book. These things happened to me and around me. I consider these the perks of the business some funny some sad and some that will stay with me the rest of my life. When you start working in the business keep a log I wish I did because now I have forgotten more than I remember. Someday maybe you will write a book. Anyway here are the stories. I hope you enjoy them.

Let's start with a horror story. Some very good friends of mine wanted to make a movie. It was really the wife more than the husband. She had delusions of grandeur and saw herself as this talented producer writer actress. She gave new meaning to the phrase jack-of-all-trades master of none. The husband on the other hand was a talented actor. He was best known as Mindy's father on Mork and Mindy and several other films. He has a marvelous sense of humor and was my friend for many years. He is a very good musician as well as an actor and I really liked him in The Buddy Holly Story. I became very close to these people over the years and gave them the honor of becoming godparents to one of my children. The wife had talked for years about making a movie from a script she wrote. She went everywhere to try to raise money to make the film. The script was mediocre at best and therefore she was unsuccessful in raising funds. Now she and her husband decided to put up their own money to make this film. I had told them for months that I did not want to work on this film and they should never put up their own money. I told them that they were going to lose their money and I did not want to be a part of it. Finally one afternoon they called me up and begged me to help produce this film and protect their interest. After we talked for a while and against my better judgment I told them I would be one of two producers on the film. The other producer was someone a mutual acquaintance had introduced us to. He had produced low budget films and knew what was involved.

The shoot was a nightmare. The show was so low budget we shot places without permits and pulled many tricks just to finish it. Usually the unions will try to organize a non-union film. This picture was so low budget they said it could not be done union and did not even try. But I did my best. I called in many favors and got lots of product placement. Adidas C and R clothiers and even a friend of mine Brad Anderson, Sly Stallones wardrobe man, gave us things for the film that wasn't in our budget. As favors to the producers we had George Siegel, Elliot Gould, Dirk Benedict, and Bo Hopkins staring in the picture and working for scale. I turned down a good paying job to help out my friends complete this project. After the picture was over I immediately went on to another show. Because my salary was all deferred (This means I get paid once the picture is released and starts to make money.) I needed to work and pay my bills. When I came back from location I get a call from the wife where she proceeded to tell me how I hurt her picture because I did not do the sound. I tried to explain that her picture was way down on the food chain and all it could do is hurt my career it certainly wasn't going to help it. There is a limit to what a friend should expect from another friend. Then she proceeded to tell me what a lousy producer I was. This came from a woman who couldn't even get her car on the set on time for a shot.

She of course didn't want to see what I was saying was true and was only concerned about her movie. So much for friendship. When we hung up we were still on good terms although from my point of view a little strained. Now the trades come out with this ad for the picture. She was trying to get a distributor to release her picture. She had the credits as follows. Her name as executive producer her name as writer her name as an actress her name and the other fellow as producer and my name nowhere to be found. I guess with her name in so many places there wasn't room for mine. So as far as loyalty in the business goes it is only there when it is convenient. Even the godparents of my child screwed me. I knew better than to get involved but I felt I could save my friends from some people taking advantage of them and in two cases I did. The end result is that I didn't get paid yes that's right they stiffed me and I spent several months of my life with the production instead of my family or working on a legitimate show. I will really miss the husband because we had a lot in common and he has a wonderful sense of humor. His wife wears the pants in that family and I'm don't have the time for wanna be's.

After I did Die Hard two I started working on a picture called the Marrying Man. This picture got a lot of publicity for two reasons. This was the picture that led to Alec Baldwin and Kim Bassinger to get married. Secondly this was the picture that Bassinger and Baldwin had many battles with Disney. Alec had gone out of his way to meet Kim when she was working on My Stepmother Was An Alien. That meeting was personal but led to the decision for both of them to work on The Marrying Man. When they were in rehearsals and then on the film they fell in love right before my eyes and everybody else's to. We were out in the desert towing the picture vehicle with Kim and Alec in the car. In between set ups they proceeded to describe the previous nights sexual escapades and what was going to take place that evening. I immediately told both of them that I had a microphone in the car and that anybody with headphones could hear their conversations. They did not seem to care and kept on talking. She is definitely the dominant one in that relationship. Disney on the other hand was so adamant about making people comply to the Disney way of doing things that the situation got out of control. On any picture the producer, director, and actors discuss characters and what they would do and wouldn't do. On this picture they would not let Kim or Alec have much input.

This created an incredible amount of frustration on the actors and crew. The producer and the director were caught in the middle while Disney had Lawyers and agents on the set. They would make Kim and Alec comply or pay for the delays. Kim got her one wish, which was to have this one producer banned from the set. What she did not realize was that he was just an errand boy for Disney and was immediately replaced by a producer they call the hammer. This guy was a joke. He was like a drill sergeant and did not solve one problem created a few more and the set was the same. When the picture was finished Disney let it die on purpose. They did very little advertising and never pushed the picture. Disney did not just let the picture die they put it in the witness protection program. They couldn't let it become a success because that would have been good for Kim and Alec. There were many stories about Kim and Alec but for the most part I got along fine with them. To show you how frustrated Alec was I saw him grab a portable phone from a Disney executive and throw it. Then he stormed out and knocked over a camera case full of expensive lenses. Disney sent the lenses back to Panavision with explicit instructions to look very carefully to find something wrong. They weren't concerned how to solve problems only how to make this actor comply.

Neil Simon was on the set every day and would sit next to me occasionally. He wrote the script and is famous for his work in comedy. One of my favorite pictures he wrote was The Odd Couple. This part of the story may or may not be true but I wasn't there so I can't say. One day Kim got in a yelling match with the studio because she was saying her character wouldn't say a certain thing and it wasn't funny. Then in a moment of frustration she blurts out Neil Simon can't write comedy! Mr. Simon never came back on the set again. The part of the story I can say is true is that Neil never did come back after that day.   Disney had the same attitude with Kim as they did with everybody. There is the Disney way or the wrong way. A good executive would have tried to find common ground and solved the problems for the good of the show. Many things were said and done but the bottom line is both sides acted in an unprofessional manner.

Let's talk about Sly Stallone. Slys oldest and dearest friend is Tony. Tony has put on some weight over the years. Sly has been bugging him to lose weight. Now Tony is like my brother and I love the guy. So we cooked up this joke to play on Sly. The whole joke took place over about 8 months. Tony tells Sly that he is losing weight because he is listening to me. Then in the mornings I would bring this fruit plate into Slys bus and give it to Tony. It is starting to really bug Sly that his oldest friend is listening to me and not him. When we talk physical fitness Sly is the epitome of good shape. He has a full time cook who prepares special meals and on every film set he has a full gym to work out. My idea of a workout is when I have to walk to the refrigerator to get something to eat. I have a nice roll of fat to keep me warm in the winter and if they ever ban fast food I might end up on a roof with a gun. On the set of Demolition man Sly got crazy and started to yell at Tony not to listen to me but to listen to him. He grabbed my little roll of fat, which hurt like hell and made a few comments as to the shape I was in. Finally we put an end to the joke when I got a movie poster of Rambo and by computer put my face on his body. The caption over the poster read as follows. With the Tim Cooney diet plan you could look like this. Tony took it and hung it in Slys bus. When Sly came to work the next day and saw it he said Cooney hasn't got a body like that?? Hey "wait a minute" finally he realized the whole thing was a joke.

Sly is really a good guy and is not given enough credit. He is one of the more intelligent people I have met and most people don't think of him this way. If you talked art politics or history Sly would probably surprise you. He is also an excellent artist. He painted a picture of Tony and himself and gave it to Tony. Tony has it hanging over his fireplace at home. He also gave his long time driver John a painting that I know is very special to John. I wish he would have given me one. I have seen Sly help many people and you will never hear about it and I have also seen many people take advantage of him. When you are famous and rich it is hard to tell who your real friends are.

So now I am in Cortina, Italy shooting Cliffhanger. When you go on some locations the production company insists that you use local help it's cheaper. So I had brought my boom man with me from Hollywood but we had to hire a cable man locally. This guy knew nothing. It would have taken two of him to make a half-wit. In order to get to the locations everyday we would have to take our equipment and get into a helicopter and be flown to the top of some snow packed mountain top. The nagra is what we used at that time to record the sound on the show. I had told this local cable man to always put it in the case for transport. He seemed to think holding it on his lap was a better idea. Sure enough on one trip he dropped it out of the helicopter. When I fired him on the spot his only concern was getting a crew jacket with the name of the film on it.

There were times on that film where the weather was very dangerous. We were working at very high elevations. On one mountain we were 16000 ft above sea level. What would happen is the clouds would roll in and the safety officers would make us go into these little building to get out of the weather. One time as we were headed for shelter I looked over at my Boom man Todd Bassman and his hair was standing straight up. There was so much electricity in the air that even one of the metal railings were humming. Lightning strikes were very common so there were no dull moments on Cliffhanger.

Then there was the time I was very lucky and actually got a film I wanted to do. Usually you go after films because you need the work in this case I really believed in the project. The film was titled "The Last days". This was a long form documentary where we took holocaust survivors back to Auschwitz, Bergen, Belson, and Dacha. We interviewed them and they told us what happened to them and what it was like to live that nightmare. I normally don't do documentaries but I had such an interest in this project because of the content I was happy to get it. One of the people we interviewed for the film was congressman Tom Lantos. He is the only congressman ever to be elected to Congress that was a holocaust survivor. We went to Washington where he took me to lunch in the private congressman's restaurant in the capitol building. We also went to Budapest, where Raul Wallenberg saved him from the camps. I was honored to stand on the floor of congress in Budapest with the great Tom Lantos. Tom passed away recently but his two children gave him a wonderful gift. They are both married and told Congressman and his wife who was also a survivor that they were going to have as many children as they could because he and his wife had lost there entire family to the Nazis. We did one shot where his entire family of children grandchildren and great grandchildren are all playing in the backyard. I quit counting at 15. I really never found out how many he had. I only mention all of it here because out of all the work I have done in over 30 years this is the picture I am the proudest of. By the way it won the Oscar and deservedly so.

I am sitting at home when the phone rings and it is my friend Angie Cobb. She is a production coordinator and at the present time working for Michael Mann. She is calling because she knows I have connections in Cuba. Michael Mann has just been turned down by the U.S. government to go to Cuba. He wanted to take the cast for research for his film Miami Vice. Which he was getting ready to shoot. I told her I could get Michael and the cast into Cuba the next day and all I wanted was an interview to do the movie. So the next afternoon Michael Mann and the cast of Miami Vice are sitting in the Hotel Nacional drinking Cubra libres and I am waiting for my interview. To this day I am still waiting I never got the interview, but I know how the business works and I will probably get something down the road. At least that's the rationalization. Also you have to ask yourself do I really want to work for Michael Mann?

Another short and sweet Cliffhanger story. We are in Rome shooting on the stage. Across the way they are making a commercial. My local Rome cable man Palo tells me Fellini is directing and if he was not doing this he would be working on the commercial because he always works with Fellini. Janine Turner and I talk Palo into introducing us. Fellini is sitting in his chair and when Palo says this is my boss I am working for on Cliffhanger he says hello I am Frederico Fellini. Janine asked for an autograph and he signed his name on an apple box. Janine dragged that box all over Europe on her way home. The man was a true gentleman.

Not to long ago I worked on a film in India. We were shooting at the palace in Rajasthan. This place was something else. A lot of gold and jewels everywhere. We were informed that the queen would be making her way down to the set. We were told of the protocols and what to do and not do according to the traditions of the country. I am not always the one to follow rules and I kind of flirted with the queen and when she asked me if I was flirting with her and I said yes but I meant it as a compliment. To make a long story a little shorter I hit it off with the queen and was invited to a party to meet the king. Now whenever I leave the United States I always take a bag of brand new baseballs with me to give to kids on the street wherever I go. So when I went to the party I was to be introduced to the king and his wife the queen who I had met the day before. When I got to the front of the line the queen whispered something into the kings ear. The king then asked me if I was the one flirting with his wife. I told him yes but it was meant as a compliment and please don't have my head cut off. Then I told him I realized in his country cricket was the game of choice because of the English influence in that country. I told him in America baseball is considered the national past time and I wanted him to have a regulation baseball as a small gesture on my part and thanks for the invitation to the party. The palace we were shooting in was unbelievable, Huge and gold everywhere. There was gold chains, statues, ceilings, furniture, pretty much gold everywhere. I was afraid to stand still because they might have covered me in gold. So a few weeks later we get a notice that the queen will be coming back to the set and please remember the protocols especially you Tim Cooney. When she arrives she makes a beeline for me. I told her it was nice to see her again when she says I have to tell you something. She says in her bedroom the king and her have a safe for there personal items. She said ever since the party right before the king goes to bed he opens the safe and takes out the baseball and looks at it plays with it a little and then puts it back in the safe. She then told me anytime I come to India I am to be their guest at the palace and to stay with them. I always thought it was interesting that a man who had all this wealth huge palace gold everywhere finds a four dollar baseball fascinating.

A guy I know calls me and says he is in this directors program and wants me to mix the sound on his short film. I usually don't do those because I already have a pretty good career going and those short films won't help your career at all. They usually don't pay much and its always long hours. Because the guy was a friend and the schedule was just two weeks I did it anyway. Much of the shooting was done in a record recording studio so it was pretty easy. One day they said tomorrow we can't shoot in studio one because BB King will be recording in there. The next day I get to work two hours early because I want to meet BB and I have a great only one of two blues guitars made by Rickenbaker. I own one and the other is in the Rickenbaker museum. When I get there and walk into the studio they said BB was already done and not there. I was pretty bummed out but when I walked into the kitchen there he was. He was just sitting there eating a sandwich and I went up to him introduced myself. I told him about the guitar and handed it to him. He started playing it and he handed me Lucile his guitar and I sat in that kitchen playing music with BB King. When we were done he gave me a little pin that is in the shape of a guitar that says BB King on it and a lifetime backstage pass to wherever he is playing. This was truly a dream come true for me. By the way the picture was called session man and won the Oscar for best short film.

When I talk to people about the business they always ask what is your favorite show. Who is your favorite actor or who is the worse? I will start this by saying many actors give back to society and you never hear about it. Sly Stallone has given money to some good causes but you never hear about it. My all time favorite is Danny Glover. I have done 3 pictures with him and I hope I get to do more. When Danny is not working he has spent his time traveling to many places to give inspirational talks to teens to stay off drugs focus on a career and Danny has paid for it out of his own pocket. When Clinton was president he made Danny a good will ambassador to Africa and he did some good work there as well. He is definitely the guy I respect the most and if you ever get to work with him consider yourself lucky I do.

Here's a quick one. I was working on a film called Paparazzi. Mel Gibson's company produced it and Mel did a cameo in it. Now Mel loves jokes but you can never get him he is too clever. I won't say whom because he probably would like to work again put a license plate frame on Mel's car that said "out of the closet and proud of it". When Mel found out he laughed and acknowledged that someone had finally got him. The trouble was it was one of those laughs that you didn't really know if he was happy or not. It was still a good joke and I have since played it on other people.

I had worked with this second AD named Allen. He was a great guy but he loved playing jokes on me and I have been known to have played a few on him. Well we were doing Murder She Wrote I think it was either the second or third season. Allen had finally made the move from second AD to first AD. We were shooting in Medicino Calif. Medicino doubles for the fictitious town of Cabot Cove Main. Now you must understand Allen's demeanor. He is efficient and a little hyper. He pays attention to every detail, which was good. On the first day of shooting we had this big parade to shoot, which had lots of background a marching band ECT. The police department that handled the crowd control and traffic was delegated to the California highway patrol. I knew several of the officers from the other times we shot up there and had spent days off with them when we would go to the range and shoot. I figured this was the perfect set up to get Allen. So here is what I did. I put a wireless microphone on my policeman friend Mac. As they are getting ready to call lunch I had one of my guys hand Allen a new walkie-talkie and told him his was not working. Allen then called lunch and everyone went to the lunchroom except me. I pushed my sound cart next to the building as my policeman friend went in to give what could have been an Oscar performance. Allen was sitting at the table eating and as Mac walked up to him I had a girl call for him on the radio. When he pulled his walkie out to respond there was a little packet with white powder attached to the bottom of Allen's walkie. Mac grabs the packet opens it and takes a taste. Now keep in mind I am outside recording this whole scenario. He says "Allen this is the real stuff you better come with me." They start walking outside and Allen looks like a dog going to the pound. He says to Allen "where did you get this" Allen says someone gave me a new walkie right before lunch. Mac says you have the right to remain silent you have the right to an attorney ECT. Ect. And reads him his rights. Mac says do you understand your rights and Allen says yes. Mac then asks him again where did you get the blow. He says he doesn't know who gave it to him. Mac says okay we have to go downtown. Allen freaks out he says it's my first day as a first AD and I can't leave. Mac says well then you better tell me where you got this. Allen immediately says TIM COONEY! He rolled over on me like a politician on a two-dollar hooker. Mac then said Tim Cooney the sound mixer Allen said yes Mac he's no good. Mac told him well if you are a friend of Tim Cooney just forget about the whole thing. Allen first was shocked and then it slowly dawned on him that I had gotten him. The best part was I recorded the entire joke and played it back over and over many times. He tried to get me back by having the special effects guy set a smoke bomb to my sound cart but I did not freak out so his joke kind of bombed. Allen is still a first AD and one of the best around. I have not worked with him since then and I hope that changes before I retire.

Lets talk about Michael Landon. Many things have been written about him but the bottom line is he was the best when it came to caring about his crew. From the producers to the drivers Michael was the best. He treated everybody like they were his family. This story comes to me from a boom man and my friend Bill Shotland who worked for Michael. When Bill first went to work on highway to heaven the show was on location. So at the end of the day the entire cast and crew went down to the bar at the hotel. Billie is single and he is sitting there talking to some local girl. Michael Landon has been known to play a few jokes in his time and this time was no different. The next day Billie comes into work and everybody on the show shuns him. Every single person tells him to stay away from them and don't come near them. So all morning know one will talk to Billie and by the way he is the nicest guy in the world. Now Billie is starting to go crazy trying to figure out what he did to piss everybody off. Just about then the girl he was talking to in the bar last night shows up on the set. He try's to talk to her but she won't talk to him either. Now it's getting close to lunchtime and Billie figures he better just move on and leave the show. He goes to the mixer he's working with and tells him he is quitting the show. The mixer told him no because it's Michaels show and he has to go clear it with him. They call lunch and Bill heads to Landon's trailer. When he gets to Michael's trailer he sees the girl he was talking to at the bar outside Michael's trailer walks by her and knocks on the door. Michael tells him to come in and Bill says Mr. Landon I have somehow managed to piss off everyone on the show and I don't even know what I have done. So I have decided to leave the show thank you for everything it was a pleasure working for you. Michael then starts asking questions. Tell me were you in the bar last night? Billie says yes. Were you talking to that girl who is standing outside right now? Billie says yes. Did you tell her you were a producer on the show and she could have a part on my TV series? Billie says no I told her I worked in the sound department. Well she is here and says she is supposed to be on MY show. Now Billie is really panicked and starts saying he did not tell her that I don't know where she got that idea and just about the time he is on the verge of tears Michael Landon's wife says Michael that's enough. He then walks up to Billie gives him a hug and says welcome to the family. Everybody on the show was in on it and from what I have heard it really was like a family there. It's hard to have that kind of fun anymore unless the star of the show sets that tone. Most of the time you are just trying to make your day.

Back in the 70s studios really had power. Presidents used to hang out with Lew Wasserman who was the head of Universal. If there was a threat of a strike Lew would step in and that was the end of it. Out of all the studios Universal was the most powerful of all of them. Universal calls me one day and says a sound guy hurt himself and am I available to fly to Hawaii. I tell them no problem and they say get to LAX to catch a plane in 3 hours. I throw a weeks worth of clothes in a bag leave a note for my wife that says went to Hawaii call you later and head to the airport. When I get there the ticket is waiting and I get checked in and eventually get on the plane. As we start to taxi and get out to the runway the captain comes on the intercom and says would Tim Cooney make himself known to the stewardess. Now post 911 they know the name of every person in every seat and now they are called flight attendants. I get up and walk down the aisle and every eye is on me like I just picked their pockets. When I get up front where the stewardess was she says Universal called and said they don't need you and we are turning the plane around. So the plane stops heading out to the runway and goes back to the terminal gets my luggage off of the plane and

I go back home. That's power. I call the sound department who sent me in the first place and they tell me the boom man who I was going to replace seems to be okay. They tell me I get paid for the day and thank you. The next day I get the same call go to the same airport get on the same plane with the same flight crew who had a few interesting comments for me and this time I actually make it to Hawaii. I was on that show for 2 months. I guess the boom man was not okay.

This story falls under the no matter how hard you try you really need to know the language category. The show is Shogun a mini series staring Richard Chamberlin. The entire show was shot in Japan in 1980 and there always seemed to be translation issues. We have ways of doing things in the film business and there are reasons why we do them. On this show we had about 30 or 40 torches. The prop guys had to light them and extinguish them as needed without holding up the show. In order to accomplish this The Hollywood prop guy would take a trashcan and put dry ice in it. He took the time to show the local Japanese guys that worked for him that if they just put the lit torches in the can the torches would just go out. He then said to them "This is the Hollywood way". Now the Japanese prop guys thought this was the greatest thing they had ever seen. They would stand there and play around putting the torches in slow and then fast just to see when the torches would go out. They were totally fascinated. The prop mater had to go into town to get some more trashcans so they could have several places to put the torches out and when he comes back he had a lovely surprise waiting for him. All the torches were sopping wet and laid out on the side of a hill in the sun. These torches were not going to be lit anytime in the next week. All his Japanese prop guys were standing there just as proud as peacocks. When the prop man tried to ask them with broken Japanese the prop men told him very proudly this is the Japanese way!

I think the funniest Shogun story was this. In the era of this story they had old musket type rifles. Well each one had to be hand loaded and it took the prop guys about 40 minutes to get them all loaded. What this meant is you would shoot one take then you would have 40 minutes to wait until all the rifles were loaded again for the next take. So the prop guys had just loaded all the rifles and were handing them to the actors and background while the translator was telling them in Japanese to not fire the weapon until this man pointing to Jerry London the director says FIRE! Jerry London was talking to the first AD explaining something to him and not really listening to the translator. Again the translator says no matter what do not shoot until this man says fire. Now Jerry says to the translator okay tell them this. When this actor does this I will say fire ….the weapon. The minute he said fire all 40 rifles went off. We had a 40-minute break.

One final note on Shogun. They were digging these trenches because they had an earthquake scene in the show. While the workers were digging one of the trenches collapsed and 2 guys were buried. Everybody stopped working and dug them out. One guy was okay but the other guy was not in good shape and was sent to the hospital. When the American crew turned around everybody else was gone. Apparently when there is an accident on the set in Japan and somebody gets hurt everybody just goes home.

On Cliffhanger we had been working many hours in Cortina Italy where a little more than half of the picture was shot. Not only did we have a lot of work to do in those cold mountains but also it never really got dark until 11 o'clock at night. We would start at 7am but would not wrap until after 9. Now months later we are moving to the stage in Rome where there is a different film union. On the first day of shooting at 6pm in the middle of a setup the lights go off. The union guys said it was time to go home. I loved it but the company worked out something with them and we worked what was considered normal for film hours. The nice thing was we only worked 5 days a week. Usually on location you work 6.

Ford Fairlane the film I had the most fun working on. Andrew Dice Clay was a character. It was funny everyday on that set and Dice and I became friends on that picture. At that time he was a star. He was selling out venues of 40 to 50 thousand seats. He comped me at one of his shows in LA and was terrific. Three standing ovations later the show was over. I go backstage to say good show and thanks. He is in his dressing room and his wife says to everybody in the hall just wait a few minutes and we could all come in. Now waiting in the hall is every important studio head, producer and agent in Hollywood. In a few minutes everybody piles into the dressing room as we wait for Dice to come out. I am standing in the back of the room and am a little intimidated by the Hollywood power brokers in the room. Dice steps out from behind a door looks around the room sees all of the Hollywood big shots. He immediately pushes past them comes up to me and says Timmy good to see you shakes my hand says thanks for coming. To me this was the classiest guy in Hollywood. A side note to this story is

I traded the prop guy on the show for the guitar Dice plays in the movie. Dice signed it for me at the end of the film. Whenever I run into Dice he always gives me the business about having the guitar because he really wanted it. The next time I see him I will probably give it to him.

This isn't a story but it occurred to me that you might want to know this. If you have ever watched the credits on a film and if you have read this entire book you now probably will just to get to know the names of people to contact. After some of the names of some of the people you might have noticed some initials. After my name you will see C.A.S. there is also A.S.C. M.P.S.E. B.S.C. C.S.C. just to name a few. What these are are organizations within the film community. They are specific to a branch of the business. C.A.S. stands for Cinema audio society. A.S.C. stands for American screen

Cinematographers. M.P.S.E. stands for motion picture sound editors. Anyway you get the picture. Sometimes the only way in is to be asked and or sponsored. Usually you have to have been doing it for along time and have a body of good work. I am a proud member of the Cinema Audio society, which is dedicated to the advancement of sound in the motion picture business. We raise money every year and donate to the ear institute charity and with all the new digital technology it can be a good way to keep up. I sat on the board twice which is a non-paid position and you are elected which is kind of a bittersweet honor but it's always good to give back when you can. So after my name it says C.A.S. We give out awards every year for what the sound community thinks is the best sound of the year. M.P.S.E. gives out there award which is called the golden Reel. They actually give one to production mixers as well as editors and I was nominated three times for their award and won one in 2000. All the organizations give out similar awards every year and if you are lucky you get to wear that tuxedo to more than one dinner.

So Okay I have saved the best for last. Die Hard Two. The party from hell. Just writing it on paper sends chills up my spine. It sends chills because to this day this picture remains as the toughest picture and also the coldest I have done and I have had some doozies. Some of my doozies include Cliffhanger, Deep Blue Sea, Demolition Man, and We Were Soldiers All difficult for different reasons. But Die Hard Two is in a twisted cold place all of it's own. First of all pause here and think of any problem you have ever had. On Die Hard Two we had them all. Anything that can go wrong on a film did and sometimes in Biblical proportions. I don't even know where to start. I can tell you this. This film had the most people ever hired for a film. At the end of the film the UPM (unit production manager) told me he ended up with over 500 deal memos just for the teamsters. Usually there might be 30 to 50 at the most. Joel Silver produced this film. Joel is one of the most accomplished producers in the business and the first time I met him he was a PA. It was the late 70s and I was a boom man at Universal on a picture called The Incredible Shrinking Woman staring Lily Tomlin. Joel was a PA at that time for Larry Gordon. Joel went from PA to one of the biggest producers in Hollywood and no one has more respect for him than I do. I watched Joel get pictures produced that no one else could. Joel could do anybody's job on or off of the set and very few producers can these days. But anyway back to the picture from hell Die Hard Two. We worked hard and long hours in many different places in this country. What I will do is just hit one or two of the twenty plus high points. First off we were chasing snow in the warmest winter ever recorded in the history of the United States. This one show holds my personal record for the most hours worked in a week 123 hours. We had to find a place where there was a runway covered in snow so that we could land a 747. One of the places we went was a place called Moses Lake in the state of Washington. The best pickup line at all the bars in Moses Lake is "nice tooth". The day before we left LA it was 25 degrees and snowing in Moses Lake. When we landed the sun was shining and it was 70 degrees and no snow. So the producers decided we would shoot inside the hanger next to the 747 while they tacked down white plastic along the runway to look like snow. We walk into the hanger and there it was this huge 747 specially painted for the film. The director and I are walking side by side when he stops and says Tim there is something wrong with the plane but he can't figure out what it is. He asks me can if I tell what's wrong. Before I can say anything thank god he sees it. They painted and sent the wrong plane. This plane is a cargo plane so it has no windows. We can't shoot it. Joel Silver has the stand by painter trying to paint windows on the plane. Yeah that 'ill work. So while that's going on they decide to shoot the swat team arriving at the hanger.

We had already shot the swat team in the blowing snow in Denver. So they bring in the swat vehicle to load the swat team and when the swat vehicle comes in its painted desert camo instead of forest camo, which won't match what we shot in Denver. So we can't shoot that. So now the heads of all the departments load into a van and drive out to the runway to look at the white plastic that has been tacked next to the runway to look like snow. WRONG! A major wind has come up and there is white plastic blowing everywhere. Joel Silver turns to the DP Oliver Wood and asks if he can shoot this. He says no it doesn't look like snow it look like plastic blowing in the wind. Joel then says Quote "They didn't go to the moon to shoot star wars" unquote."

Well by now it's about 5am and they wrap and we go back to the Moses lake inn and tire center. About 7am I wander downstairs because I don't sleep well in hotels and I was still not unwound from the party we call production. When I get down to the lobby the second AD is there saying come on lets go. I ask him what he is talking about. Apparently someone forgot to call me. The production is sending everybody back to LA and Joel Silver wanted all the department heads on a plane in an hour. So I rush upstairs to throw my stuff in a suitcase and then called my boom man and cable guy. The good news is we are going home the bad news is they have to gather all the walkies on the show. Back then it was the sound departments responsibility to handle the walkies. On that show we had over 500 and it took them 10 hours to find them all. While my guys are in walkie-talkie hell with no sleep I am headed to the Moses Lake airport hair care and jiffy mart. It felt like the last plane out of Saigon. Little did we no that would be the one of easiest days on the show.

While the company was on the road they had moved refrigeration units on the stage because they wanted to see Bruce's breath on film. It was 25 degrees on stage and 90 plus outside on the Fox lot. Coats on Coats off no danger of catching pneumonia or at the very least a cold there. Well there wasn't enough humidity in the air so you could not see any breath from anybody. All they did was make it an uncomfortable place to work. We used the ever-popular Senhisers 416 and 816 Good Humor mics for the dialog on the stage. Joel comes in one morning and says he found an airport in the snow where we could land a 747. The next day we are on are way to Alpena Michigan where moss grows on the north side of people.

To this day it is the coldest place I have ever been. Oh I forgot to mention we had over two months of solid nights and in Michigan it was 35 below all night long. The guys on the crew were opening bottles of water and pouring them slowly and watching, as the water would freeze before it hit the ground. Cameras and nagras froze even with heaters blowing on them. I really should have opened up that vet taxidermy clinic. So we are working all night long night after freezing cold night. We are shooting one of the final scenes where the 747 rolls up after landing. The doors open Bonnie Bedilia walks out of the plane door as people are sliding down the emergency chute. She sees Bruce at the bottom of the ramp smiles slides down the chute into his arms. That's what was supposed to happen. Here's the way it really went.

We are on at least our 6th meal penalty it is 3 in the morning it has warmed up to a balmy 34 degrees and instead of snow it is raining. Because of the rain the paint on the 747 is running off of the jet like its going through a car wash. They had painted the plane with water base paint. Joel has got one standby painter on an easy lift trying to paint a 747 and get the paint back on. The rain is winning without a fight. Terry Miller the first AD tells Joel we should just break for lunch and hope the rain stops. Joel who has been known to raise his voice on occasion says no one on this entire film is ever going to eat again and just roll the #%*@! Cameras. There were six cameras. The cameras were rolling the 747 comes taxing into its spot the rain had stopped kind of, the back door opens. The emergency chute unfolds and extras start sliding down the chute. The front door opens and all we heard was a pop. The emergency chute instead of unfolding came unattached from the plane and went shooting across the runway in a big square package. Terry Miller turns looks at Joel picks up his walkie and says that's lunch. It would take about 2 hours to reattach the chute to the plane.   If you ever see the last scene of the film you can see Hawaiian Air coming through at the top of the plane. There were so many more stories but I could write a book just about that one film.

Chapter 10

It's a Wrap

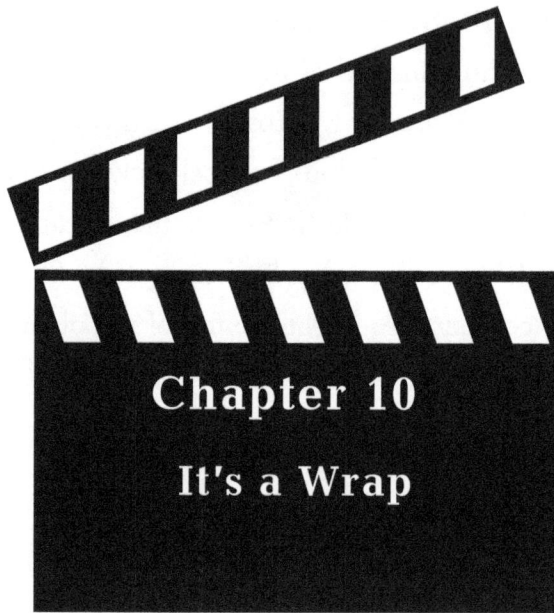

O kay so let's sum up what we have learned. Knock on lots of doors and be willing to work for anybody that will hire you. If you want to go into production and you can afford to work for free do it. Otherwise go to film school even if it is at your local college and develop relationships. If you want to direct try to get into one of the programs and no matter what keep writing. Should you want to work in the technical side of the business try a related field to get your foot in the door. The key is if you want it bad enough you won't give up. The business is set up so only the persistent make it.

Don't forget to make your own Luck. Be in the right places you need to be to meet the right people and the right situations. One thing I have noticed about the younger generation. That is apathy. We could not afford to be apathetic or someone else would get hired. Do your best possible work EVERYTIME! You will be a big success and I will end up working for you.

Here are some of the phrases and terms used in this business. Once you know what they are these sentences won't sound so bizarre.

Rip the eye out of that baby and hang it by its head on a trombone!

Kill the baby strike the midget hang the black!

1. "Grip" A grip is a person who places nets and other diffusion in front of lights. He builds dolly tracks for the camera and any other on set construction. He also rigs any camera mounts.

2. "Gaffer" A gaffer is the guy in charge of lighting the set and works hand in hand with the cameraman or D.P. as he is called.

3. "Grifflon ,gel scrims" These are all various diffusions that go in front of lights to get the right lighting effect.

4. "One k five k ten k" These are various sizes of lights.

5. "Key grip and best boy" The key grip is the grip in charge and the best boy is the second in charge the best boy is in charge of the equipment.

6. "Barney" A barney is a cover that goes over the camera to reduce noise.

7. "Mag" A mag is short for magazine that holds the film in the camera.

8. "Insert car" An insert car is a specially built truck that tows picture vehicles and has places to mount cameras at various positions.

9. "Two ot four ot" These are different sizes of cables.

10. "Singles doubles" These are different sizes of diffusion that go in front of or in lights.

11. "Teeny midget baby" These are different size lights.

12. "Gaffer tape" This tape looks similar to duct tape but is made out of cloth and is much stronger.

13. "Trombone maryjane" These are brackets that you can mount lights on.

14. "Slate" The slate is used for the editors to have a visual cue so that they can take the sound track which is separate and sync it up with the picture either by the sound the slate makes when it is slapped or by the time code that is shown on the slate and is on the sound as well. Now they use time code

15. "High roller c-stand" These are various stands that hold diffusion and flags.

16. "Nagra" This is the machine that records the entire dialog when they are shooting in the old days now we use digital machine of various kinds.

17. "Dolly track, boards" These are set up by the grips to put the camera on so it can move during the shot.

18. "Abbey singer" This is the second to last shot of the day.

19. "Riser" This is a device that will raise the camera up to various levels on the mount.

20. "Apple box" This is a wooden box that comes in various sizes and is used for various reasons.

21. "Boom" The boom is what the microphone is attached to.

22. "Groveler" This is a pad that you kneel on.

23. "Barn door" This a set of metal doors that is attached to lights so you can block the light off of certain parts of the set.

24. "Eye brow" This is a shade that fits on to the front of the camera to take the light out of the lense.

25. "Squeezer" This is a variac control to dim lights.

26. "Two tees" This is a term for the size of a particular shot. It is short for teeth and tits.

27. "Cowboy" This is a term for the size of a particular shot. The bottom frame would be about where a cowboy would wear his guns.

28. "Obie light" This is an eye light attached to the camera.

29. "Zeppelin" This is a basket like device that the microphone goes into to protect it from the wind.

30. "Cutter teaser black flag" These are a black solid flags that grips set to take light off certain parts of the set.

31. "Cuckoloris" This is a piece of wood with holes in it that goes in front of a light to give the set a special light effect.

32. "Stinger" This is an extension cord.

33. "Furny pad" This is short for furniture pad it is a blanket.

34. "Black wrap" Black metal foil that goes right on the lights to protect set pieces from light and heat.

35. "Off set arm, side arm" Metal arms that hold lights at different than normal angles.

36. "Martini shot" Last shot of the day.

37. "Cow catcher pork chop" These are boards that attach to the camera dolly to give the operator and assistant an easier and larger place to work.

38. "Video assist" This is video equipment attached to the camera so after a shot the director can see the last take and decide whether to do another take.

39. "Playback" This is music that is played so the actors can lip sync or dance when they are shooting.

40. "Eye" This is the glass lense that is in front of the actual light bulb on various lights

41. "Head" this is a light that is not attached to a stand

42. "Abby Singer" Abby is a real person when he was a first AD he always used to say this is the last shot when he knew he had 2 or 3 to go. I guess he thought everybody would work faster if they thought they were almost finished for the day. So the second to last shot is always called "The Abby" or Abby Singer

43. "The "Martini" is always the last shot of the work day because the shot after that is in your glass

Here is an article I wrote for the Cinema Audio Society magazine. The article was meant to be funny but there are a lot of truths in this article. I just put it in the book because I thought you would enjoy it.

The Interview
Or
How Did I Get
This Job?

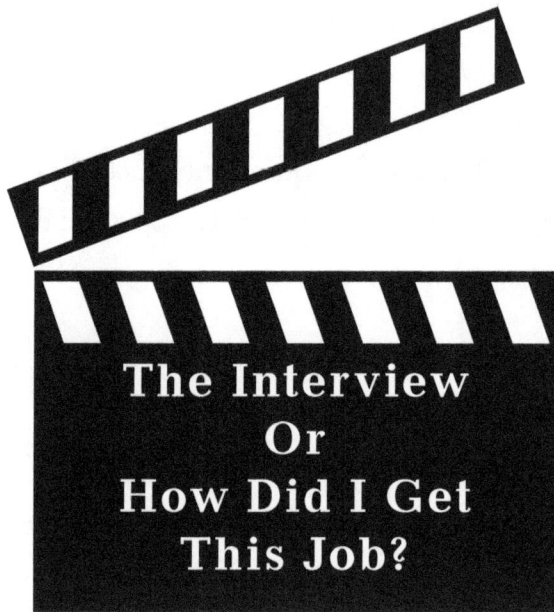

Although this is grossly exaggerated for your reading pleasure, all of the following events actually happened. I have changed the names of the films involved to protect the innocent, which by the way is me. I would like to get hired by these people again.

So I am an out-of-work production mixer who has been sitting at home wondering how to pay my bills and wondering if I will ever work again. Just as my train of thought was in the neighborhood of how to get on The Price Is Right or American Idol to try and pick up a few bucks, the phone rings. A voice on the other end asks if I am available and if I can come in tomorrow at two o'clock to meet the director and the producer. I jump at this opportunity like Oprah on a Christmas ham. I tell them it would be my pleasure and I get directions. Just as the voice is going to hang up I ask the name of the film. The voice says the film is called Ten Million Cold French Nights and hangs up. Already I have broken two of my own filmmaking rules. Number one, never take a film with "night" in the title and number two, never work "French" hours unless you're in France. So I express my concern to my "at the time" wife. She reminds me that I need to take this job because she still has a black belt in shopping to maintain. Just then my 18-year-old daughter comes in and informs us that she has been accepted to the only college in the United States that does not have a scholarship program. Before I can even respond my son comes walking in and lets us know that the only college he is planning on attending is clown. All of a sudden, Ten Million Cold French Nights is starting to look better, and I have not had the interview yet. I try to convince my "then wife" she could really help out the financial situation if she were to get a little part-time job. After all, she is just sleeping between midnight and five o'clock and I am sure I could get her a paper route. She didn't go for it so I got ready for the interview. French Nights or no French Nights.

I decide it would be prudent to go over my resume. During the last interview, the director said and I quote, " Oh, you mixed the sound on that picture? That was my favorite picture when I was in junior high." I did not get that job but later I saw the picture that he directed and I think his talents really lay in the fast-food industry. Anyway, I check my resume, calculate when someone might have gotten out of junior high and high school, and was a

PA for two years and then became a director. I take everything off of my resume before that time frame, hopeful I will convince the director and producer I don't have one foot in the Motion Picture and Television Home. I have the name of the director and decide to go to IMDB to see what he has done. I see this guy is fairly new and has only directed one other film! Who would a thought? The film was a huge success. It was entitled Teenage Hitch hiking Sleezebitches From Outer Space. The picture was made for $2.7 million and made $107 million not including DVDs. As I scan through the credits, of his last film, I see many of the same people are doing the same film that I am interviewing for tomorrow. Two things immediately come to mind. Number one, why are they not highering the mixer who did his first picture and number two, why did they call me—I don't know any of these people. Now you might figure since this director's picture made so much money, a big windfall, they would have a really good budget on this one. Wrong! I am absolutely positive when I get to the interview I am going to hear, we really don't have a lot of money. The company is on the verge of bankruptcy. And furthermore, if they cant keep the budget down, they will have to take the picture to Montreal. Now for those of you out there that don't know me, some people do not find me very diplomatic. It is truly one of my faults that I have been working on my whole life. So I must reminded myself, I must not tell them that Montréal is just Mexico with an accent. Actually it is well known in the industry that if Switzerland ever goes to war, it will directly or indirectly be my fault. Well now, it's too late to rent this guys one-and-only film, so I do the next best thing. I call my kids in and ask them if they have seen this picture. My kids are like Cliff notes for movies. Their attention spans and Cliff notes are defiantly in the same ballpark. Luckily, the boy says it's his favorite movie. Next week it will be something else but for now I am in luck. He proceeds to tell me about the movie, hopefully he gets it right. Now maybe I can meet this director and have something to talk about- some common ground.

I arrive for the interview 15 minuets early and I am told that the director is still in a meeting. In Hollywood, everybody is in a meeting. If you go to the ATM machine, you are in a meeting with your banker. At that moment I wish I were in a meeting with my Plummer. I don't do interviews well. Up on the wall behind this persons desk is a shooting calendar schedule. There is not one damn day on it, the whole film will be shot at night except for the last week. In the last week, there is a holiday, which works because then they can turn us around to shoot the last week during the daylight. Now as I sit there waiting my turn I am thinking, I should have listened to my mom. I would have had my own parish by now but what's done is done. I make small talk with the person at the desk to try to find out more about the director and producer until it's my turn. Now the door opens and out comes the mixer who just won the Oscar a few weeks ago. We say hi, I congratulate him on the Oscar and he tells me good luck. I walk into the office and meet the director and the producer. Immediately they tell me the reason I am there. I played music in a band with a producer who was friends with the director. Keep in mind that this picture has no music, no playback, no bar scene with a jukebox, nada!! Just your typical dialogue-type picture. I try breaking the ice if asking if they would like the production tracks recorded to a DVD or digital tape or would they prefer analog. I tell them I have the capability to do both. They look at me like the RCA dog. They have no idea what I am talking about. Then I notice artwork in this guys-office so I switch gears and make a nice comment about some painting behind his desk. He ask me if I am interested in art and have I ever been to the Getty museum? I tell him no cause they don't have the painting I like there. He asks me which on is that? I tell him you know, the one with dogs playing poker. Once again he looks at me strange. So I tell him I did see the Mona Lisa in Paris a couple years ago but he's not buying it. Luckily for me, at that moment I spot a guitar in the corner and ask him about it. The director proceeds to tell me about his music and the songs he wrote, ETC. He asks me if I write songs and where I get my inspiration for my lyrics in my songs. I tell him most of my inspirations come from restraining orders. Finally, after a half hour of him telling me about the music he likes and his favorite bands and traveling down memory lane the interview is over. They say thanks for coming in, thanks for your time, ETC... Now I am the one who looks like the RCA. Dog. We never talk about the show or the sound on the show or anything to do with the show. So I figure that's it. I blew it and I don't have a chance that they will pick me for the gig. As I am in my car on the way home the cell rings and it's the show I just interviewed for. They ask me if I can come back cause they have decided to go with me. As a matter of fact, they ask me to hold on for the UPM. Who needs to discuss the rates with me. I try and think back an hour or so and try to figure out when I crossed over that bridge to the Twilight Zone. When the UPM comes on the phone. The first thing this guy says is although I don't know you, I am happy you are going to be doing our picture. Now we don't have a lot of money because the company is small. We are doing everything we can to not take this to Canada (I use my restraint not to tell him the accent thing) and by the way, we can't pay your usual rate. Of course he does not have a clue what my " usual rate" is, he just knows he cant pay it. At this point I pull over to the curb and hang up. Sure enough, two minutes later the phone rings and it's the UPM saying sorry we got disconnected. I told him, " Actually, we did not get disconnected. When you said you could not pay my 'usual rate', and you did not even know what it was, I figured we had nothing to talk about and I hung up." There was this 20 seconds of silence and I was not going to speak first. Finally he says, " Look, the producer and the director really like (to this day I don't know why) please come back to the office." When I get back to the office, the UPM is waiting for me. We sit down and worked everything out. Since then I have done two more pictures with these guys. On the second picture I did with the director, I decided to try and figure out this interview process we have to go through. I asked him why he asked me over the other mixers when he did not know me. All he said was, " I liked your energy" I wish I knew what the hell that meant. I would use it again. According to "my then wife", I have very little energy. But I am not going to discuss my shortcomings here.

I would say about half of my interviews go like this one where they don't talk about the show or what they want or what they expect. The other half are fairly normal and they know exactly what they want. What the criteria is for landing the job is beyond me. I have been doing these interviews for 30 years, and I still don't know what the answer is. If some one out there does know, please clue the rest of us in. I think what the deal is, if they don't have a particular mixer in mind, they interview you to find out if they can live with you for two or three months. After all, they think anybody can do the job so It's about your personality. It sad that experience or recognition (like nominations and awards) won't even get you the interview. I have had mixers in the post who are going to mix the picture, recommended me for the job, and even that didn't get me the interview. Of course, we have all run in to the producers cousin who has just bought the latest equipment and has done one commercial. So lets go with him because of the we-will-save-money-syndrome. But then I have done an $80 million picture with a director who has only done one commercial. So now I have to finish this article because believe it or not, I am on my way to an interview. I feel pretty confidant. I have been to the Getty and I have been told that this director is an animal activist and really into French culture. So I have to hurry to go to my sister's house and pick up her French poodle to take with me. Who knows, maybe he will like my energy.

Order this book online at www.trafford.com
or email orders@trafford.com

Most Trafford titles are also available at major online book retailers.

Note for Librarians: A cataloguing record for this book is available from Library and Archives Canada at www.collectionscanada.ca/amicus/index-e.html

Printed in Victoria, BC, Canada.

ISBN: 978-1-4269-1531-4 (soft)
ISBN: 978-1-4269-1532-1 (hard)

Library of Congress Control Number: 2009933238

Our mission is to efficiently provide the world's finest, most comprehensive book publishing service, enabling every author to experience success. To find out how to publish your book, your way, and have it available worldwide, visit us online at www.trafford.com

Trafford rev. 9/10/2009

Trafford
PUBLISHING® www.trafford.com

North America & international
toll-free: 1 888 232 4444 (USA & Canada)
phone: 250 383 6864 ♦ fax: 812 355 4082